Real Reading 1

Real Reading 1

Creating an Authentic Reading Experience
Lynn Bonesteel

Lynn Bonesteel
Series Editor

Paul Nation
Series Consultant

PEARSON
Longman

Real Reading 1: Creating an Authentic Reading Experience

Pearson Education, 10 Bank Street, White Plains, NY 10606

Staff credits: The people who made up the **Real Reading 1** team, representing editorial, production, design, and manufacturing, are Nancy Flaggman, Ann France, Dana Klinek, Amy McCormick, Robert Ruvo, Debbie Sistino, and Jennifer Stem.

Cover art: Shutterstock.com
Text composition: TSI Graphics
Text font: Helvetica Neue
Illustrations: TSI Graphics—pages 21, 47, 77, 82, 96, 101, 125; Gary Torrisi—pages 12, 113, 155, 163, 164, 169
References: see page xx
Credits: see page xxiii

Library of Congress Cataloging-in-Publication Data

Bonesteel, Lynn.
  Real reading : creating an authentic reading experience / Lynn Bonesteel.
       p. cm.
  Includes index.
  ISBN-10: 0-13-606654-2 (Level 1)
  ISBN-10: 0-13-814627-6 (Level 2)
  ISBN-10: 0-13-714443-1 (Level 3)
  ISBN-10: 0-13-502771-3 (Level 4)
  [etc.]
  1. English language--Textbooks for foreign speakers. 2. Reading comprehension.
  3. Vocabulary. I. Title.
  PE1128.B6243 2010
  428.6'4--dc22

                                                    2010017172

PEARSON LONGMAN ON THE WEB

Pearsonlongman.com offers online resources for teachers. Access our Companion Websites, our online catalog, and our local offices around the world.

Visit us at **pearsonlongman.com**.

ISBN 10: 0-13-606654-2
ISBN 13: 978-0-13-606654-5

Printed in the United States of America
1 2 3 4 5 6 7 8 9 10—V011—15 14 13 12 11 10

CONTENTS

Acknowledgments

I would like to express my appreciation to all of those at Pearson who made this project possible. Special thanks to Dana Klinek for her hard work and efforts to keep all of the pieces moving in the right direction; to Pietro Alongi for believing in the project in the first place; to Debbie Sistino for always being there when support was needed; to editors Martha McGaughey and Joan Poole for their hard work and careful attention to detail; and to Associate Managing Editor Robert Ruvo, Senior Art Director Ann France, and Photo Research Manager Aerin Csigay.

I was also fortunate to have the opportunity to work with two wonderful writers, Alice Savage and David Wiese. Their hard work, creativity, flexibility, and good humor made the collaboration a pleasure.

Finally, I would like to thank Paul Nation, whose contributions from the inception of the project to its completion were invaluable. His explanation of the authentic reading experience during an online TESOL seminar served as the spark that led to the creation of the *Real Reading* series. His ongoing feedback was instrumental in the design and content of many of the exercises in the four books of the series. Our goal was to create a reading series informed by solid research on second language acquisition. Where we have succeeded, much of the credit belongs to Paul Nation and other researchers who make their work accessible to teachers and materials writers. By doing so, they perform an invaluable service to language learners.

Lynn Bonesteel

Reviewers

William Brazda, Long Beach City College, Long Beach, CA; **Abigail Brown**, University of Hawaii, Honolulu, HI; **David Dahnke**, North Harris Community College, Houston, TX; **Scott Fisher**, Sungshin Women's University, Seoul, Korea; **Roberta Hodges**, Sonoma State American Language Institute, Sonoma, CA; **Kate Johnson**, Union County College Institute For Intensive English, Elizabeth, NJ; **Thomas Justice**, North Shore Community College, Danvers, MA; **Michael McCollister**, Feng Chia University, Taiching, Taiwan; **Myra Medina**, Miami-Dade Community College, Miami, FL; **Lesley Morgan**, West Virginia University, Morgantown, WV; **Angela Parrino**, Hunter College, New York, NY; **Christine Sharpe**, Howard Community College, Columbia, MD; **Christine Tierney**, Houston Community College, Houston, TX; **Kerry Vrabel**, GateWay Community College, Phoenix, AZ.

INTRODUCTION

Real Reading 1 is the first book in a four-level (beginning, low intermediate, intermediate, and high intermediate) intensive reading series for learners of English. The books in the series feature high-interest readings that have been carefully written or adapted from authentic sources to allow effective comprehension by learners at each level. The aim is for learners to be able to engage with the content in a meaningful and authentic way, as readers do in their native language. For example, learners who use *Real Reading* will be able to read to learn or feel something new, to evaluate information and ideas, to experience or share an emotion, to see something from a new perspective, or simply to get pleasure from reading in English. High-interest topics include superstitions, shyness, neuroscience, sports, magic, and technology, among others.

> THE *REAL READING* APPROACH

To allow for effective comprehension, the vocabulary in the readings in the *Real Reading* series has been controlled so that 95-98 percent of the words are likely to be known by a typical learner at each level. The vocabulary choices were based on analyses of the General Service Word List (GSL) (Michael West, 1953), the Academic Word List (AWL) (Averil Coxhead, 2000), and the Billuroğlu-Neufeld List (BNL) (Ali Billuroğlu and Steve Neufeld, 2007).

Research has shown that as they read a text, good readers employ a variety of skills.[1] Thus, essential reading skills, such as predicting, skimming, making inferences, and understanding text references, are presented, practiced, and recycled in each level of *Real Reading*, with level-appropriate explanations and practice. The goal is for learners to become autonomous readers in English; the reading skills are the tools that will help learners achieve this goal.

Vocabulary development skills and strategies are prominently featured in every chapter in *Real Reading*. The importance of vocabulary size to reading comprehension and fluency has been well documented in the research on both first and second language acquisition.[2] Thus, in the *Real Reading* series, learners are given extensive practice in applying level-appropriate skills and strategies to their acquisition of the target words in each chapter. This practice serves two purposes: First, because the target words have been selected from among the most frequent words in general and academic English, learners who use the books are exposed to the words that they will encounter most frequently in English texts. Second, through repeated practice with vocabulary skills and learning strategies, learners will acquire the tools they need to continue expanding their vocabulary long after completing the books in the series.

---

[1] Nation, I.S.P. *Learning Vocabulary in Another Language.* Cambridge, England: Cambridge University Press. 2001.

[2] Nation, I.S.P. *Teaching Vocabulary: Strategies and Techniques.* Boston, MA: Heinle, Cengage Learning. 2008.

VOCABULARY: FROM RESEARCH TO PRACTICE
By Paul Nation

Real Reading puts several well-established vocabulary-based principles into practice.

1. There is the idea that meaning-focused input should contain a small amount of unknown vocabulary but that this amount should be limited so that the learners can read for understanding without being overburdened by a large number of unknown words. Research suggests that somewhere around two percent of the running words in a text may be initially unknown and still allow a reasonable level of comprehension. If the number of unknown words is too large, then the learners cannot participate in an authentic reading experience. That is, they cannot read the text and react in the same way as a native speaker would. The texts in *Real Reading* have been developed so that learners are likely to gain a high level of comprehension while encountering some new words that they can begin to learn.

2. The activities in *Real Reading*, along with the texts, provide learners with the opportunity to thoughtfully process the unknown vocabulary that they encounter. In most of the exercises, the contexts for the target words are different from the contexts provided in the texts. This helps stretch the meaning of the new words and makes them more memorable. The various exercises also require the target words to be used in ways that will help learning.

3. *Real Reading* includes a systematic approach to the development of important vocabulary learning strategies. The ultimate goal of instructed vocabulary learning should be to help learners become autonomous language learners. An important step in this process is gaining control of effective vocabulary learning strategies, such as using word cards, using word parts, and using a dictionary. *Real Reading* includes vocabulary strategies in every unit. The strategies are broken down into their components, practiced and recycled in the vocabulary practice pages at the back of the books.

4. The sequencing of the vocabulary in *Real Reading* has been carefully designed so that the new items will not interfere with each other. That is, presenting the target words together with new vocabulary that belongs to the same lexical set or consists of opposites or synonyms greatly increases the difficulty of vocabulary learning. It is much more helpful if the unknown vocabulary fits together in ways that are similar to the ways the words occur in the texts.

5. Finally, a well-balanced language course provides four major kinds of opportunities for vocabulary learning. A unique feature of *Real Reading* is its use of these research-based principles. First, there is the opportunity to learn through *meaning-focused input*, where the learners' attention is focused on the message of what they are reading or listening to. Second, there is an opportunity to learn through *meaning-focused output*, where the learners are intent on conveying messages. Third, there is the opportunity to learn through *language-focused learning*, where learners give deliberate attention to language features. Fourth, there is the opportunity to *develop fluency* with what is already known. In a variety of ways, the *Real Reading* textbooks provide these opportunities. Their main focus is on deliberate learning through conscious attention to vocabulary, and through the use of specially designed exercises.

THE *REAL READING* UNIT

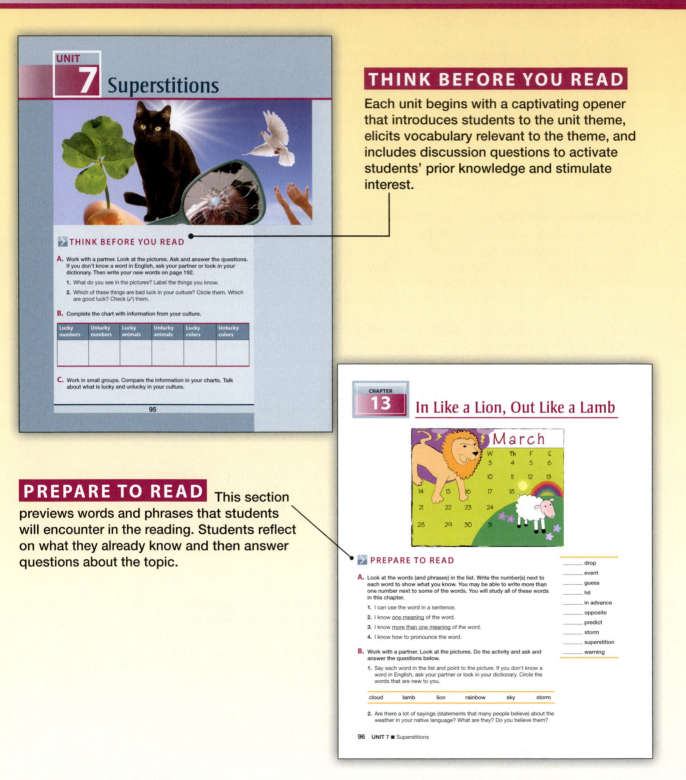

THINK BEFORE YOU READ

Each unit begins with a captivating opener that introduces students to the unit theme, elicits vocabulary relevant to the theme, and includes discussion questions to activate students' prior knowledge and stimulate interest.

PREPARE TO READ This section previews words and phrases that students will encounter in the reading. Students reflect on what they already know and then answer questions about the topic.

The inset pages show:

UNIT 7 Superstitions — page 95

> THINK BEFORE YOU READ
>
> **A.** Work with a partner. Look at the pictures. Ask and answer the questions. If you don't know a word in English, ask your partner or look in your dictionary. Then write your new words on page 192.
>
> 1. What do you see in the pictures? Label the things you know.
> 2. Which of these things are bad luck in your culture? Circle them. Which are good luck? Check (✓) them.
>
> **B.** Complete the chart with information from your culture.
>
> | Lucky numbers | Unlucky numbers | Lucky animals | Unlucky animals | Lucky colors | Unlucky colors |
> |---|---|---|---|---|---|
> | | | | | | |
>
> **C.** Work in small groups. Compare the information in your charts. Talk about what is lucky and unlucky in your culture.

CHAPTER 13 — In Like a Lion, Out Like a Lamb — page 96

> PREPARE TO READ
>
> **A.** Look at the words (and phrases) in the list. Write the number(s) next to each word to show what you know. You may be able to write more than one number next to some of the words. You will study all of these words in this chapter.
>
> 1. I can use the word in a sentence.
> 2. I know one meaning of the word.
> 3. I know more than one meaning of the word.
> 4. I know how to pronounce the word.
>
> _____ drop
> _____ event
> _____ guess
> _____ hit
> _____ in advance
> _____ opposite
> _____ predict
> _____ storm
> _____ superstition
> _____ warning
>
> **B.** Work with a partner. Look at the pictures. Do the activity and ask and answer the questions below.
>
> 1. Say each word in the list and point to the picture. If you don't know a word in English, ask your partner or look in your dictionary. Circle the words that are new to you.
>
> cloud   lamb   lion   rainbow   sky   storm
>
> 2. Are there a lot of sayings (statements that many people believe) about the weather in your native language? What are they? Do you believe them?
>
> **96   UNIT 7 ■ Superstitions**

READING SKILLS Every unit has one or two reading skills, which include previewing and predicting; understanding topics, main ideas, and details; and understanding cause and effect, among others.

READ The readings feature a wide variety of high-interest, contemporary topics, including business, science and nature, music and the visual arts, culture and society, sports and exercise, and health and nutrition, as well as a variety of genres, including newspaper and magazine articles, blogs, Web sites, newsletters, travel logs, personal essays, poetry, and short stories. Vocabulary is tightly controlled at each level, and target words are recycled from one chapter to the next within a unit, from unit to unit, and from one level to the next.

Reading Skill: Summarizing

To check your understanding of a reading, it can be helpful to write a *summary* of it. A summary is much shorter than the reading. It includes only the main idea, the subtopics that support the main idea, and just the most important examples or details that support the subtopics.

C. Preview the magazine article "Do Animals Lie?" Then check (✓) the main idea.

_____ 1. Birds are very good at fooling other animals.

_____ 2. Birds and chimpanzees behave in strange ways.

_____ 3. Animals sometimes act dishonestly in order to survive.

_____ 4. Chimpanzees know how to lie.

▶ **READ**

Read "Do Animals Lie?" Was your answer for Exercise C correct?

Do Animals Lie?

1 Most people agree that honesty is a good thing. But does Mother Nature agree? Animals can't talk, but can they lie in other ways? Can they lie with their bodies and behavior? Animal 5 **experts** may not call it lying, but they do agree that many animals, from birds to chimpanzees, behave dishonestly to **fool** other animals. Why? Dishonesty often helps them survive.
    Many kinds of birds are very **successful** 10 at fooling other animals. For example, a bird called the plover sometimes **pretends** to be hurt in order to protect its young. When a predator[1] gets close to its **nest**, the plover leads the predator away from the nest. How? It 15 pretends to have a broken wing.[2] The predator follows the "hurt" adult, leaving the baby birds safe in the nest.

    Another kind 20 of bird, the scrub jay, **buries** its food so it always has something to eat. Scrub jays are also **thieves**. They 25 watch where others bury their food and **steal** it. But clever scrub jays seem to know when a thief is watching them. So they go back later, unbury 30 the food, and bury it again somewhere else.
    Birds called cuckoos have found a way to have babies without doing much work. How? They don't make nests. Instead, they **sneak** into other birds' nests. Then they lay[3] their

35 eggs and fly away. When the baby birds hatch,[4] their **adoptive** parents feed them.
    Chimpanzees, or chimps, can also be sneaky. After a fight, the losing chimp will give its hand to the other. When the winning chimp 40 puts out its hand, too, the chimps are friendly again. But an animal expert once saw a losing chimp take the winner's hand and start fighting again.

    Chimps are sneaky in other ways, too. 45 When chimps find food that they love, such as bananas, it is natural for them to cry out. Then other chimps come running. But some clever chimps learn to cry very softly when they find food. That way, other chimps don't hear them, 50 and they don't need to share their food.
    As children, many of us learn the saying "You can't fool Mother Nature." But maybe you can't trust her, either.

[1] **predator:** an animal that kills and eats other animals
[2] **wing:** the part of a bird's body used for flying
[3] **lay:** make eggs come out of the body
[4] **hatch:** be born by coming out of an egg

Vocabulary Check

Write the letter of the correct definition next to the word. Be careful. There are two extra definitions.

_____ 1. adoptive   a. to put something in the ground and cover it with dirt
_____ 2. bury   b. to trick someone
_____ 3. expert   c. to do something quietly because you do not want people to see or hear you
_____ 4. fool   d. someone who steals something
_____ 5. nest   e. to hurt someone or something
_____ 6. pretend   f. responsible
_____ 7. sneak   g. a person with special skill or knowledge in a subject
_____ 8. steal   h. a place made by a bird to live in
_____ 9. successful i. to behave as if something is true when you know that it is not
_____ 10. thief   j. to take something that you do not own without asking for it
                      k. doing well
                      l. (parents) not by birth but by taking a child that is not your own into your family and raising it as your own

VOCABULARY CHECK This section gives students an opportunity to focus on the meaning of the target vocabulary before completing the comprehension activities.

THE *REAL READING* UNIT (continued)

READING GOAL
The reading goal gives students a purpose for rereading the text before completing the comprehension activities. Reading goals include completing a graphic organizer, giving an oral or written summary of a text, retelling a story, identifying the writer's point of view, and giving an opinion on the content of a text, among others.

COMPREHENSION CHECK
Engaging and varied exercises help students achieve the reading goal. Target vocabulary is recycled, giving students additional exposure to the high frequency words and expressions.

▶ READ AGAIN

Read "Folktales" again and complete the comprehension exercises. As you work, keep the reading goal in mind.

📖 **READING GOAL:** To understand the characteristics of four different kinds of folktales

Comprehension Check

A. Complete the chart. Check (✓) the characteristics of the different types of folktales.

Characteristic	Fable	Pourquoi story	Trickster tale	Fairy tale
1. magical powers				
2. a clever character				
3. animals behave like humans				
4. the main character lies				
5. usually has a happy ending				
6. a moral at the end				
7. explains something about the natural world				
8. punishment for bad behavior				

B. Think of a folktale to tell your classmates. Draw pictures on a separate sheet of paper to help you remember the story. Look up any words you need and write them under the pictures. Look at the words and pictures and practice telling your story.

C. Work in small groups. Tell your folktales. Check (✓) the characteristics in the chart for each folktale. Then write what kind of folktale you think it is. Remember, some stories have characteristics of more than one kind of folktale.

Characteristic	Student 1	Student 2	Student 3	Student 4
magical powers				
a clever character				
animals behave like humans				
the main character lies				
usually has a happy ending				
a moral at the end				
explains something about the natural world				
punishment for bad behavior				
What kind of folktale is it?				

▶ DISCUSS

Work in small groups. Ask and answer the questions.

1. What is the moral of "The Ant and the Grasshopper"? Explain your answer. (There is more than one correct answer.)

2. In your culture, do you have a story with a similar moral? What is the story? Tell it to your group.

DISCUSS
A variety of activities for small group or pair work encourages students to use vocabulary from the current unit as well as previous units.

VOCABULARY SKILL BUILDING

This section offers presentation and practice with skills such as identifying parts of speech, learning and using derived forms of target words, learning common affixes and roots, and recognizing common collocations, among others.

> ## VOCABULARY SKILL BUILDING
>
> ### Vocabulary Skill: Adjectives
>
> *Adjectives* are words that describe nouns (people, places, things, or ideas). Adjectives come in front of the nouns that they describe. They can also come after a linking verb such as *be, feel, seem, look, taste,* or *smell.*
>
> **EXAMPLES:**
>
> a *safe* city
> a *flat* table
> a *clever* idea
> He looks *relaxed.*
>
> **A.** Read the sentences. Underline the adjectives.
>
>   1. You are a very <u>clever</u> boy.
>   2. There are no waves today. The surface of the water is flat.
>   3. His legs are powerful.
>   4. After I exercise, I always feel relaxed.
>   5. I like natural food.
>   6. My mother cooked a special meal for my birthday.
>
> **B.** Work in small groups. Ask and answer the questions. Use the boldfaced adjectives in your answers.
>
>   1. When do you feel **relaxed**?
>   2. Do you have any **natural** abilities, such as a **natural** ability in music, dance, math, art, or a sport?
>   3. Is your city **safe**?
>   4. Are your feet **flat**?
>   5. Who is the **clever**est person you know?
>
> 20 UNIT 2 ■ Telling Stories

LEARN THE VOCABULARY

This final section of each unit challenges students to practice strategies and techniques outlined by Paul Nation that will help them to acquire not only the target vocabulary but also vocabulary beyond the text. Activities include learning from word cards, guessing meaning from context, discovering core meaning, using a dictionary, and learning word parts, among others.

> ## Learn the Vocabulary
>
> ### Strategy
>
> **Using Word Cards: Example Sentences**
>
> If it is hard for you to remember the meanings of the words on your cards, add an example sentence to the back of the card. You can copy the example sentence from the reading where you found the word, or you can find an example sentence in your dictionary. Make sure you copy the sentence carefully.
>
> **A.** Add an example sentence to the back of each of the cards that you made for Unit 1.
>
> **B.** Make cards for the words from Unit 2 that were new to you when you started the unit. Include target words and words that you wrote on page 191. Write an example sentence for each word.
>
> **C.** Work with a partner. Quiz each other on all of your cards (Units 1 and 2). If you can't remember a word, your partner will read the example sentence on the card but will say "blank" in place of the word. If you still can't remember the word, your partner will put that card to one side. Then have your partner quiz you on that card again after you finish all of your other cards.
>
> **EXAMPLE:**
>
> **Student A:** In a trickster tale, no one "blank" a character for bad behavior.
> **Student B:** Punishes!
> **Student A:** Yes. That's correct.
>
> **D.** Go back to the vocabulary list at the beginning of each chapter. What did you learn about the target words? Add your numbers to the list.
>
> **Vocabulary Practice 2,** see page 194
>
> UNIT 2 ■ Learn the Vocabulary 27

THE *REAL READING* UNIT (continued)

FLUENCY PRACTICE

Four fluency practice sections address learners' extensive reading needs. Learners practice fluency strategies, read passages, check comprehension, and calculate their reading times. Fluency progress charts are provided at the back of the book for students to record their reading times and Comprehension Check scores.

FLUENCY PRACTICE 4

Fluency Strategy

To become a more fluent reader, you need to read every day, and you need to read a lot. The material should be very easy for you, but you need to read many pages a week. Ask your teacher to help you find readings that are at the correct level. Graded readers—books that have been written with a simple vocabulary—are a good place to start. Again, your teacher can help you to find readers at the correct level. Set yourself a goal of a certain number of pages every week. For example, you can start by reading 25 pages a week. Then increase the number of pages by ten pages every week, so that in the second week you are reading 35 pages, 45 in the third week, and so on.

▶ READING 1

Before You Read

Scan "Twins in the News" on the next page and answer the questions.

1. What are the names of the twins in the article?

FLUENCY PRACTICE 4

	Words per Minute	
	First Try	**Second Try**
Reading 1		
Reading 2		
Comprehension Check Score _____%		

VOCABULARY PRACTICE

These pages appear at the back of the book and reinforce understanding of the target vocabulary, vocabulary skills, and vocabulary learning strategies.

VOCABULARY PRACTICE 3

THINK ABOUT MEANING

Look at the words in the list. Think about their meanings, and decide where to put them in the chart. Some of the words can go in more than one place in the chart. Be ready to explain your decisions.

Food	Training	Danger
		death

death	prepare
full	raw
license	responsible
pass	serious
poisonous	survive
practical	wild

PRACTICE A SKILL: Word Families

Look at the words in the chart. If the word doesn't have a suffix, put an *X* in the chart. If the word has a suffix, write the suffix in the second column. Then remove the suffix to make another word in the same word family. Make sure you spell the new word correctly.

Word	Suffix	Word without the suffix
1. agreement	*-ment*	*agree*
2. full	*X*	*X*
3. ground		
4. imagination		
5. scientist		
6. raw		
7. pass		
8. license		
9. dangerous		
10. poison		
11. preparation		
12. death		

PRACTICE A STRATEGY: Using Word Cards with Example Sentences

Review your word cards for this unit. If a word is difficult for you to remember, add an example sentence to the back of the card. You can copy the sentence from the reading, or you can copy an example sentence from your dictionary.

Vocabulary Practice 3   195

REAL READING COMPONENTS

- **MP3 Audio CD-ROM:** Each level has a bound-in MP3 Audio CD-ROM with recordings of all target vocabulary and readings.

- **Teacher's Manual:** The online Teacher's Manual provides a model lesson plan and includes the Student Book Answer Key. The Teacher's Manual is available at www.pearsonlongman.com/realreading.

- **Tests:** The Online Tests consist of a reading passage followed by comprehension, vocabulary, and vocabulary skill questions for each unit. An answer key is included. The Tests are available at www.pearsonlongman.com/realreading.

HOW TO USE THE LESSON PLAN

Overview of Unit Format

Each unit of Real Reading 1 consists of two thematically related chapters. Compelling readings in a variety of genres have been carefully written or adapted from authentic sources and feature a principled approach to vocabulary development.

- Chapters consist of pre-reading and post-reading activities, including a reading skill, a reading goal, comprehension questions, and discussion activities.
- Reading and vocabulary skill building and vocabulary learning strategies based on Paul Nation's research help students become more confident and successful in preparation for academic reading and reading on standardized tests.

Suggested Methods of Instruction

This lesson plan can serve as a generic guide for any chapter in the student book.

- Suggested methods for delivering instruction for each section or activity in a chapter are presented.
- Alternative ways to handle each activity are provided under the heading *Variations*. These options allow instructors to vary the way they treat the same activity from chapter to chapter and in so doing to identify the methods that work best for a specific class or individual students.

Think Before You Read

The activities in this section are designed to prepare students for the topics, themes, and key vocabulary in the readings.

A. and B. *(approximately 10 minutes)*

1. Give students a few minutes to read the discussion questions. Answer any questions.
2. Have students form pairs to discuss their answers. Tell them they will report at least one of their answers to the class.

After 10 minutes, ask several students to share their answers.

Variations

- After students have discussed the questions, ask them to write for 1–3 minutes in answer to the questions. Have students exchange their writing with a partner or group member and compare their ideas.
- Ask students to answer the discussion questions in writing at home. Have them read their partner's or group members' answers in class and discuss their answers.
- Assign one discussion question per pair or small group. Have each pair or group discuss the question and report their ideas to the class.
- Choose one discussion question and have each student do a one-minute freewrite to expand ideas generated from the discussion. The students' writing can be passed around the class or reviewed in small groups to encourage further feedback and discussion. The activity may also serve as a closure to the discussion.

Real Reading Teacher's Guide 1

NAME: _____ DATE: _____ SCORE _____ /40

UNIT 1
TEST

Synchronized Swimming

It's part swimming, part gymnastics, and part dance. It's synchronized swimming, one of the more unusual sports in the Olympic Games. Many people love to watch it. The swimmers move their bodies in and out, forward and back, on the surface and under water. They move in perfect time with each other and the music.

Synchronized swimming was first called "water ballet." It's easy to see why. It's like ballet. And like ballet, it seems easy, but it isn't. The swimmers seem natural and relaxed, but they have to train for a long time. Many exercises are done under water, so they have to hold their breath for as long as two minutes. It takes a lot of strength, power, and energy.

Synchronized swimming first began in Europe in the 1890s. At that time, swimmers often trained outside, in rivers or in lakes. The first synchronized swimmers were men. But by the middle of the 20th century, most synchronized swimmers were women. Swimmers sometimes performed in the theater, where they swam in large water tanks on the stage! Later, some Hollywood musicals used synchronized swimmers. The actress Esther Williams starred in movies such as *Bathing Beauty* in 1944 and *Million Dollar Mermaid* in 1952.

Synchronized swimming became an Olympic sport in 1984. In the Olympic Games, swimmers work in teams of nine athletes, or in pairs. They show their skills by doing special movements above and below the water. They do not touch the bottom of the pool. Instead, they move their hands like flippers and kick their feet. This helps them stay up in the water. Like all Olympic athletes, they work very hard. Their dream is the same: to win a medal for their country in the Olympic Games.

Part 1

Comprehension

Circle the letter of the correct answer to complete each sentence.

1. In the Olympics, synchronized swimming is done _____.
   a. on land   b. to music   c. by one person
2. According to the article, synchronized swimming looks _____.
   a. easy   b. difficult   c. dangerous
3. Swimmers have to hold their breath because they need to _____.
   a. be underwater   b. train outside   c. swim on the surface
4. Synchronized swimming was first done by _____.
   a. children   b. men   c. women
5. In the early part of the twentieth century, people watched synchronized swimming _____.
   a. in the Olympics   b. in the theater   c. at the beach
6. In the Olympics, the swimmers cannot _____.
   a. kick their feet b. move their hands   c. touch the bottom

   Total: ____ / 6

2 *Real Reading Tests*

SCOPE AND SEQUENCE

Unit	Chapter	Reading Skill
1 In the Water	**1** Just Add Water	Previewing and Predicting
	2 Phelps's Feet	
2 Telling Stories	**3** Folktales	Understanding Topics
	4 Anansi and Turtle	Understanding Sequence
3 What's for Dinner?	**5** Dangerous Dining	Scanning
	6 Wild Treasures	Understanding Details
Fluency Practice 1	**Reading 1** The Gift, Part 1	
	Reading 2 The Gift, Part 2	
4 Funny Business	**7** The Science of Laughter	Active Reading
	8 Can't Take a Joke	Understanding the Main Idea
5 Some of My Best Friends Are Animals	**9** The Best-Dressed Penguin	Understanding Pronouns
	10 Christian the Lion	
6 Learning from Mother Nature	**11** Natural by Design	Understanding Examples
	12 Swarm Intelligence	Visualizing
Fluency Practice 2	**Reading 1** Pinky the Duck, Part 1	
	Reading 2 Pinky the Duck, Part 2	

Vocabulary Skill	Vocabulary Strategy
Nouns and Verbs	Deciding Which Words to Learn: Making Word Cards
Adjectives	Using Word Cards: Example Sentences
Word Families	Using Word Cards: Changing Order and Grouping
The Suffixes -al and -ity	Using a Dictionary
The Prefix dis-	Using a Dictionary: Verb Forms
Collocations	Using a Dictionary: Collocations

SCOPE AND SEQUENCE

Vocabulary Skill	Vocabulary Strategy
Nouns that End in *–ing*	Using a Dictionary: Finding Members of the Same Word Family
The Prefix *in-*	Figuring Out Meaning from Context
The Prefix *un-*	Using Word Parts to Guess Meaning
Phrasal Verbs	Using the Keyword Technique
Roots and Prefixes	Using Word Parts to Guess Meaning
Adjectives and Adverbs	Choosing Words to Learn

References

Anansi and Turtle. (n.d.). *Motherland Nigeria.* Retrieved from
http://www.motherlandnigeria.com/stories/anansi_and_turtle.html

Barrand, O. (2008, Sept. 17). *Evolution favours superstitious beliefs.* Retrieved from
Cosmos Online: http://cosmosmagazine.com

Batten, M. (2006, October). *Do animals lie?* Retrieved from BNET:
http://findarticles.com/p/articles/mi_qa4128/is_200610/ai_n17194550

Bell, R. (n.d.). *Skywayman: The story of Frank W. Abagnale Jr.* Retrieved from
http://www.trutv.com/library/crime/criminal_mind/scams/frank_abagnale/index.html

Bird, W. (2008, August 24). Natural by design: "Biomimicry" creates sustainable technology
from the fruits of evolution. Retrieved from The Japan Times Online: http://japantimes.co.jp

Burgdorf, J., & Pankseppa, J. (2003, April 17). "Laughing" rats and the evolutionary
antecedents of human joy? [Electronic version] *Physiology & Behavior, 79,* 533–547.

Cardenas, J. (2007, July 6). Path of most resistance: For a really fulfilling workout, gym-
goers are abandoning their exercise bikes and taking to the water. *South China Morning
Post.* Supplements, p. 30.

Cheong, J. (2008, April 30). Jump into the pool for gentler workouts: Water-based exercises
are low-impact and suit all ages. *The Strait Times, Singapore.*

Collins, T. (2008, Oct. 17). Fraudster Frank Abagnale criticizes UK card scheme.
Retrieved from ComputerWeekly.com: http://www.computerweekly.com

Conan, N. (2007, Oct. 25). Strangers become sisters as twins reunite. *Talk of the Nation.*
National Public Radio.

Cottrell, R. (2007, Sept. 15). *But it's OK, they're here to help you.* Retrieved from
More Intelligent Life: http://www.moreintelligentlife.com

de Maupassant, G. (2004) *The Project Gutenberg EBook of Maupassant Original Short
Stories (180), Complete.* Retrieved from http://www.gutenberg.net

Dearon, J. (2007, March 23). *Mushroom fanatics are crazy for fungi.* Retrieved
from USA Today: www.usatoday.com/tech/science

Flatz-Byers, R. (2008, Aug. 3). Aquatics 4 Life. Retrieved from The Aquatic Exercise
Association: http://www.aeawave.com

Folktales. (n.d.). Retrieved from Chariho Regional School District:
http://www.chariho.k12.ri.us

Frankel, M. (2000, April 24). When the tulip bubble burst. Retrieved from BusinessWeek:
http://www.businessweek.com/2000/00_17/b3678084.htm

Ganz, D., & Ganz, L. (n.d.). *Twinsworld.* Retrieved from http://www.twinsworld.com

Gonzales, Laurence. (2004). *Deep survival: Who lives, who dies, and why.* New York,
New York: W.W. Norton and Company, Inc.

Gonzalo, S. (n.d.). *MSNBC.* Twins separated at birth reunite after 15 years. Retrieved from
http://www.msnbc.msn.com/

Goodall, J. (1990). *Through a window: My thirty years with the chimpanzees of Gombe.*
London: George Weidenfield & Nicoson.

Grant, W. Ecuadorian doctors "stole twin." Retrieved from BBC News, Miami:
http://news.bbc.co.uk/2/hi/americas/6294174.stm

References

Grifantini, C. (2007, Oct. 25). Robotic swarms. *Hypercube: Science in All Dimensions.* Retrieved from http://www.bu.edu/phpbin/news-cms

Hayden, S. (n.d.). Deadly foods and liquids. suite100.com. Retrieved from http://food-facts.suite101.com

Hays, J. (n.d.). Fugu (Blowfish) in Japan. Retrieved from Facts and Details: http://factsanddetails.com

Highfield, R. (2008, October 9). Why we evolved to be superstitious. Retrieved from Telegraph.co.uk: http://www.telegraph.co.uk

Intrigue, thievery, and heartbreak… it's all in the history of the Tulip. (n.d.). *Tesselaar gardening at its best.* Retrieved from http://www.tesselaar.net.au/flowerandgarden/thetulip.asp

Koda, K. *Insights into second language reading: A cross-linguistic approach.* New York, NY: Cambridge University Press, 2004.

Lightbrown, P., & Spada, N. (2006) *How languages are learned.* Oxford, England: Oxford University Press.

Markey, S. (2005, May 23). Truffle riches drive men to secrecy, crime in Italy. Retrieved from National Geographic News: http://news.nationalgeographic.com/news

Martinez-Conde, S., & Macknik, S. (2008, Nov. 24). Magic and the brain: how magicians "trick" the mind. Retrieved from Scientific American Magazine: www.scientificamerican.com

Mercedes-Benz Bionic Concept Vehicle (2005, June 7). Retrieved from http://www.worldcarfans.com

Montgomery, S. (1991). *Walking with the Great Apes: Jane Goodall, Dian Fossey, Birute Galdikas.* New York, New York: Houghton Mifflin Company.

Moore, V. (2007, May 5). The lion in my living room. *Daily Mail (London). Ed. 1st,* p. 50.

Nation, I.S.P. (2001) *Learning Vocabulary in Another Language.* Cambridge, England: Cambridge University Press.

Nation, I.S.P. (2008) *Teaching Vocabulary: Strategies and Techniques.* Boston, MA: Heinle, Cengage Learning.

O'Connell, C. (2008, Feb. 11). Now you see me….*The Irish Times,* Innovation, p. 28.

Platt, A. (2008, April 27) To die for. Retrieved from New York Magazine: http://nymag.com/restaurants/features/46462

Prince, A. (2008, Aug. 13). The science behind swimmers' dolphin kick. Retrieved from NPR.org: http://www.npr.org

Psychology of survival (2002, May). *U.S. Army Field Manual,* Ch. 2, FM 3-05.70 [FM21-76]. RK19 Bielefeld Mitte. Retrieved from http://rk19-bielefeld-mitte.de/survival/FM/02.htm

Ralston, A. (2004) *Between a Rock and a Hard Place.* New York, New York: Atria Books.

Researchers: It's easy to plant false memories. (2003, Feb. 16). Retrieved from CNN: http://www.cnn.com

Siegel, R. (2007, Oct. 25). "Identical strangers" explore nature vs. nurture. *National Public Radio, All Things Considered.*

Siegel, R. (2008, April 25). Pierre sheds wetsuit for real penguin suit. *National Public Radio, All Things Considered.*

References

Sohn, E. (2004, Nov. 3). Inspired by nature. Retrieved from http://www.sciencenewsforkids.org

Spencer, R.E. (1954, Dec. 27). Weekly weather and crop bulletin. Retrieved from http://usatoday.com/weather/wproverb.htm

Swan, N. (2000, March 17). Frank Abagnale—new life. Retrieved from http://anlimara.tripod.com/abagnaleintervw.html

Tennant, D. (2007, November 1). Frank Abagnale breaks his silence. Retrieved from http://www.itbusiness.ca

Then and Now: Aron Ralston. (2005, June 19). Retrieved from CNN: http://www.cnn.com

Tulipomania. (n.d.). *History House: An Irreverent History Magazine.* Retrieved from http://www.historyhouse.com/in_histor2005y/tulip

United Cerebral Palsy (2008, Sept. 27). *Exercise & Fitness: Aquatic Therapy.* Retrieved from http://www.ucp.org

Videnieks, M. (2007, Oct. 2). Wet ways to get fit. *The West Australian (Perth)*, Metro p.1.

Walker, N. (n.d.). Weather Proverbs: True or False? Retrieved from http://wxdude.com

Waller, J. (2008, Sept. 18). Falling down. Retrieved from The Guardian: http://www.guardian.co.uk

Where tulips come from. (n.d.). Retrieved from http://www.bulb.com

Wilson, J. (n.d.). *Skywatch: Signs of the weather*. Retrieved from http://wilstar.com

Zimmer, Carl. (2007, Nov. 13). From ants to people, an instinct to swarm. *The New York Times*, p. F1.

Photo Credits

Page 1 Shutterstock.com; **p. 2** (left) Shutterstock.com, (right) Shutterstock.com; **p. 8** (left) Shutterstock.com, (right) AP Images/Mark Baker; **p. 10** (1) Shutterstock.com, (2) Shutterstock.com, (3) Purestock/Photolibrary, (4) Shutterstock.com, (5) Shutterstock.com; **p. 14** The Art Archive/Kharbine-Tapabor; **p. 15** Clipart.com/Jupiterimages; **p. 23** (1) Shutterstock.com, (2) Shutterstock.com, (3) Shutterstock.com, (4) Shutterstock.com; **p. 24** (5) Dreamstime.com, (6) Shutterstock.com, (7 left) Shutterstock.com, (7 right) Shutterstock.com; **p. 28** Shutterstock.com; **p. 29** Shutterstock.com; **p. 34** Paolo Siccardi/age fotostock; **p. 46** www.CartoonStock.com; **p. 48** Shutterstock.com; **p. 53** www.CartoonStock.com; **p. 54** Chuck Savage/Corbis; **p. 59** Shutterstock.com; **p. 60** AP Images/Eric Risberg; **p. 61** Shutterstock.com; **p. 74** Dreamstime.com; **p. 75** (left) Photo courtesy of DaimlerChrysler AG, (right) Photo courtesy of DaimlerChrysler AG; **p. 79** (1) Shutterstock.com, (2) Bill Bachman/Alamy; **p. 80** (3) Shutterstock.com, (4) Shutterstock.com; **p. 81** Creatas/Photolibrary; **p. 85** (left) Blickwinkel/Alamy, (right) Bill Gozansky/Alamy; **p. 86** Shutterstock.com; **p. 95** Shutterstock.com; **p. 103** Shutterstock.com; **p. 109** Shutterstock.com; **p. 110** Michael O'Neill/Corbis Outline; **p. 112** Shutterstock.com; **p. 116** Brendan McDermid/Reuters/Landov; **p. 124** Spencer Grant/PhotoEdit Inc.; **p. 126** Tim Davis/Corbis; **p. 130** DreamWorks/Photofest; **p. 139** Shutterstock.com; **p. 144** Rick Gershon/Getty Images; **p. 145** (left) Shutterstock.com, (right) Photo courtesy of Karol and Karen Groom; **p. 150** Elena Seibert/Corbis Outline; **p. 157** (left) Library of Congress, (middle) Mary Evans Picture Library/The Image Works, (right) iStockphoto.com; **p. 158** (left) Warner Bros./Photofest, (middle) Sebastian D'Souza/AFP/Getty Images, (right) Bigstockphoto.com; **p. 164** Corbis RF/Alamy; **p. 172** Universal Pictures/Photofest; **p. 173** Shutterstock.com.

Text Credits

Page 90, 92–93 "Pinky the Duck" from *Pet Miracles: Inspirational True Tales of Our Beloved Animal Companions* by Brad Steiger and Sherry Hansen Steiger. Used by permission of Adams Media Corporation. **p. 146** Adapted from "Seeing Double" by Dea Birkett in *The Guardian*, Saturday, July 9, 2005. Used by permission.

In the Water

› THINK BEFORE YOU READ

A. Work with a partner. Look at the picture. Ask and answer the questions. If you don't know a word in English, ask your partner or look in your dictionary. Then write your new words on page 191.

   1. Where is the woman in the picture?

   2. What is she doing?

B. Work with a partner. Ask and answer the questions.

   1. Do you know how to swim? If not, would you like to learn?

   2. Do you play any sports? Which one(s)?

CHAPTER 1

Just Add Water

> PREPARE TO READ

A. Look at the words in the list. Write the number(s) next to each word to show what you know. You may be able to write more than one number next to some of the words. You will study all of these words in this chapter.

1. I can use the word in a sentence.

2. I know <u>one meaning</u> of the word.

3. I know <u>more than one meaning</u> of the word.

4. I know how to pronounce the word.

B. Work with a partner. Look at the pictures. Ask and answer the questions. If you don't know a word in English, ask your partner or look in your dictionary. Then write your new words on page 191.

1. Where are the people in the pictures? What are they doing?

2. Do you like to exercise? Why or why not?

3. What kinds of exercise do you do?

_____ advantage

_____ body

_____ burn

_____ energy

_____ exercise

_____ land

_____ relaxed

_____ safe

_____ training

_____ weigh

Before you read something, first get a general idea about the topic by *previewing*. To preview, look at the title and any pictures. For a short article, read the first sentence of every paragraph and the last sentence of the last paragraph. Then try to guess, or *predict*, what the reading will be about.

C. Preview the magazine article "Just Add Water." Then answer the questions.

   1. What kind of exercise is the reading about?

   2. Who can do this kind of exercise?

   3. What is one advantage of this kind of exercise?

 **READ**

Read "Just Add Water." Underline the answers to the questions for Exercise C.

Just Add Water

1 Are you looking for a new way to **exercise**? Do you want to keep cool while you **burn** calories?[1] If you answered yes, maybe it's time to get out of the gym[2] and into the pool.

5 More and more people of all ages are trying aquatic exercise. Aquatic exercise is like exercise on **land**, but you do it in a swimming pool. For example, you can run, walk, and do aerobics[3] or yoga.[4]

10 There are many **advantages** to aquatic exercise. Your **body** is lighter in the water. You **weigh** 90 percent less in the pool than at the gym. That's why exercising in the pool feels easier. But you burn the same number of calories 15 as at the gym. That's because it takes more **energy** to move in the water.

Aquatic exercise is also **safe** and easy to learn. For most kinds of aquatic exercise, you don't even need to know how to swim. You 20 don't need much **training**. You can do it at any age. You can do it safely with an injury[5] or when you are pregnant.[6] You can move in ways that are not possible on land. Some people who cannot walk on land can walk and even run in 25 the water.

All exercise is good for you, but aquatic exercise has one more important advantage. Most people feel more **relaxed** when they are in the water. And that means they will 30 probably exercise more.

---

[1] **calorie:** a unit for measuring the amount of energy a food can produce

[2] **gym:** a large room where you do exercises or training

[3] **aerobics:** exercise that you do with music

[4] **yoga:** a system of exercises to relax you and make you stronger

[5] **injury:** damage to the body, often from exercise

[6] **pregnant:** carrying a baby inside your body

Vocabulary Check

Complete the sentences with the boldfaced words from the reading.

1. Swimming, running, and walking are different ways that you can _____.

2. You look very thin. How much do you _____?

3. Swimming is good for your _____. It is very good for your arms and legs. It is also good for your heart.

4. Exercising in a pool has many _____ over exercising in a gym.

5. After I exercise, I take a hot shower. Then I feel very _____. It's a nice feeling.

6. When you exercise, you _____ calories. That helps you lose weight.

7. You should eat before you exercise. Your body needs _____.

8. I don't like the water. I like to run and do yoga on _____.

9. Running on land isn't always _____. You can fall and get hurt.

10. If you want to teach an aerobics class, you will need some _____. You will have to take classes and read books about exercise.

READ AGAIN

Read "Just Add Water" again and complete the comprehension exercises. As you work, keep the reading goal in mind.

> 📖 **READING GOAL:** To explain what aquatic exercise is and why it is a good way to exercise

Comprehension Check

A. Circle the letter of the correct answer to complete each sentence. There is only one correct answer.

1. Aquatic exercise is _____.
  a. done in the water
  b. difficult to learn
  c. not safe for older people

2. Your body stays cool when you _____.
  a. run on land
  b. exercise in the gym
  c. do aquatic exercise

3. Your body is lighter in the water than on land, so _____.
  a. it feels easier to move in the water
  b. you don't burn calories when you exercise
  c. you lose more weight when you exercise on land

4. When you do aquatic exercise, you don't need _____.
  a. to know how to swim
  b. a swimming pool
  c. energy

5. To learn how to do aquatic exercise, you need _____.
  a. a lot of training
  b. water
  c. a teacher

6. Sometimes people who can't walk on land can _____.
  a. run in the water
  b. walk in the gym
  c. weigh more in the water

B. Answer the questions. Try not to look back at the reading.

1. What is aquatic exercise? _____

    a. Who does it? _____

    b. Where do they do it? _____

    c. What do they do? _____

2. What are some advantages of aquatic exercise? List three.

    _____

    _____

    _____

C. Now look back at the reading. Check your answers for Exercise B. Correct any mistakes.

> **DISCUSS**

Work in small groups. Ask and answer the questions.

1. Have you ever done aquatic exercise? If not, would you like to try it?

2. Choose two activities that the people in your group do for exercise. Fill in the chart. Compare the two activities. What are the advantages and disadvantages of each?

Activity	Advantages	Disadvantages

› VOCABULARY SKILL BUILDING

Vocabulary Skill: Nouns and Verbs

To use a word correctly, you need to know its part of speech. *Nouns* and *verbs* are the most common parts of speech in English. Every sentence has at least one noun (the subject) and one verb.

Nouns are words for people, places, things, and ideas. The word *body* is a noun.

Verbs describe actions, experiences, or states. The word *weigh* is a verb.

Some words, such as *exercise*, *burn*, and *land*, can be used as **both nouns and verbs**.

Read the sentences. Are the underlined words nouns or verbs? Write *N* for noun or *V* for verb.

_____ **1.** Aquatic <u>exercise</u> is safe.

_____ **2.** They <u>exercise</u> every day.

_____ **3.** Our bodies <u>burn</u> food for energy.

_____ **4.** I have a <u>burn</u> on my arm.

_____ **5.** If you fall off your bike, try to <u>land</u> on the grass.

_____ **6.** It is safer to run in the pool than on <u>land</u>.

Phelps's Feet

> PREPARE TO READ

A. Look at the words in the list. Write the number(s) next to each word to show what you know. You may be able to write more than one number next to some of the words. You will study all of these words in this chapter.

1. I can use the word in a sentence.

2. I know <u>one meaning</u> of the word.

3. I know <u>more than one meaning</u> of the word.

4. I know how to pronounce the word.

B. Work with a partner. Look at the pictures. Ask and answer the questions. If you don't know a word in English, ask your partner or look in your dictionary. Then write your new words on page 191.

1. What is the name for the animals in the first picture? What are they doing?

2. Who is the man in the second picture? What is in his hand?

3. Do you have any medals or awards? How did you get them?

_____ flat

_____ forward

_____ kick

_____ natural

_____ power

_____ special

_____ stretch

_____ surface

_____ wave

_____ win

C. Preview the magazine article "Phelps's Feet." Then check (✓) the questions that you think the reading will answer.

_____ **1.** Who is Phelps?

_____ **2.** How is Phelps like a dolphin?

_____ **3.** Is Phelps married?

_____ **4.** Where is Phelps from?

_____ **5.** Why is Phelps a good swimmer?

_____ **6.** Where will the next Olympics be?

❯ READ

Read "Phelps's Feet." Underline the answers to the questions that you checked (✓) for Exercise C.

Phelps's Feet

1   In the 2008 Olympics[1] in Beijing, China, swimmer Michael Phelps won eight gold medals. He was the first person to **win** so many medals in one Olympics. How did he
5   do it? It took years of training, a lot of hard work, **natural** ability, and . . . very big feet.

Phelps uses the dolphin **kick** when he swims. The dolphin kick is a **special** way of moving your feet in the water. When you
10   swim on the **surface** of the water, you make **waves**. And the waves slow you down. With the dolphin kick, a swimmer's feet are always below the surface of the water, so there are no waves. That's how dolphins swim, and

15   they are some of the fastest animals in the ocean.

Many swimmers use the dolphin kick. But Phelps has a special advantage. His feet are very large and very **flat**. They are more
20   like a dolphin's flipper[2] than most people's feet are. And his large feet give him a lot of **power**.

Phelps can also **stretch** his feet out very far, even farther than a ballet[3] dancer can.
25   That gives him a big advantage in the water. He stretches his feet out very far. He then snaps[4] them down quickly to move his body **forward**.

---

[1] **the Olympics:** an international sports event that happens every four years

[2] **flipper:** a flat part of the body of some large sea animals, used for pushing themselves through water

[3] **ballet:** a kind of dance in which a story is told with dance and music but not speaking

[4] **snap:** move into a different position very suddenly

Vocabulary Check

Look at the pictures and read the definitions. Write the target word from the list on page 8 next to the correct picture or definition.

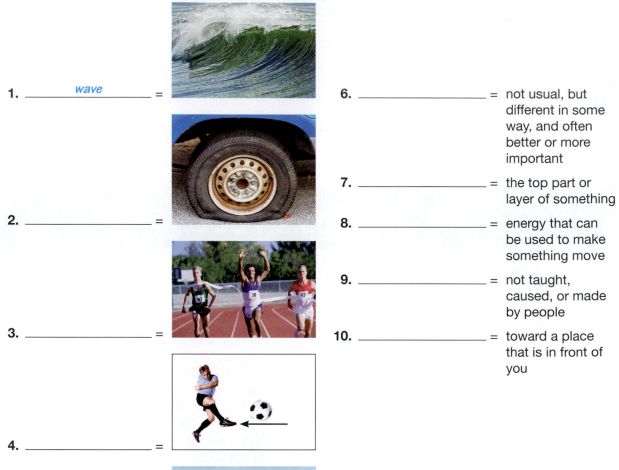

1. _____wave_____ =

2. _____ =

3. _____ =

4. _____ =

5. _____ =

6. _____ = not usual, but different in some way, and often better or more important

7. _____ = the top part or layer of something

8. _____ = energy that can be used to make something move

9. _____ = not taught, caused, or made by people

10. _____ = toward a place that is in front of you

❯ READ AGAIN

Read "Phelps's Feet" again and complete the comprehension exercises on the next page. As you work, keep the reading goal in mind.

> 📖 **READING GOAL:** To explain who Michael Phelps is and how his feet help him

Comprehension Check

A. Read the statements about the reading. Write *T* (true) or *F* (false). If it is not possible to tell, write *?*.

_____ 1. Michael Phelps is one of the fastest swimmers in the world.

_____ 2. Michael Phelps was born in China.

_____ 3. Phelps is the only swimmer who can do the dolphin kick.

_____ 4. Dolphins make a lot of waves when they swim.

_____ 5. Phelps has large feet, so he doesn't need to train very much.

_____ 6. Phelps's unusually large, flat feet give him a lot of power as a swimmer.

_____ 7. Phelps is a good ballet dancer.

_____ 8. Phelps always stretches before he swims.

B. Work with a partner. Take turns explaining (1) who Michael Phelps is and (2) how his feet help him. Check (✓) each question word as you answer those questions. Try not to look back at the reading.

_____ 1. Who?   _____ 4. How many?

_____ 2. Where?   _____ 5. How?

_____ 3. What?

C. Now look back at the reading. Did you and your partner answer the questions in Exercise B correctly?

> ## DISCUSS

Work in small groups. Complete the chart with your ideas. If you don't know a word, ask a classmate or look in your dictionary.

Sport	Body type
1. swimming	*large, flat feet*
2. basketball	
3. weightlifting	
4. soccer	

Learn the Vocabulary

Deciding Which Words to Learn: Making Word Cards

Most of the target words in this book are high-frequency words. *High frequency* means that English speakers use these words a lot. That's why you should study the words in this book carefully. Of course, you need to learn other words, too. Follow the steps below to decide which words to learn first.

When you hear or see a word you don't know, write it on the New Words pages in the back of the book, but don't try to learn it right away. If you hear or see the word again, put a check mark (✓) next to the word. Add another check mark each time you hear or see the word. When you have three check marks next to a word, it is time to learn it.

To learn a word, make a word card for it. Word cards are a very good way to learn vocabulary. It is easy to make and use them. Just follow these steps:

1. Write the new word on one side of a (4 x 6) index card.

2. On the other side of the card, write the translation in your native language, draw a picture of the word, or write the definition in English.

3. Review your cards at least once a day. When you review, look at one side of the card, and try to remember the information on the other side.

4. Say the English word out loud and spell it.

Every day, make a few new cards for the words you want to learn that day and review all of your cards. Never throw any cards away.

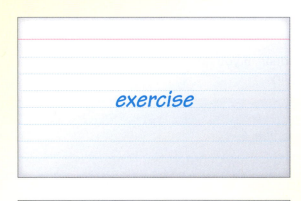

A. Make cards for the words from Chapters 1–2 that were new to you when you started the unit. Include target words and words that you wrote on page 191. Make sure you spell the new words correctly!

B. Work with a partner. Take one of your partner's cards and show him or her the back side of it (the side with the translation, drawing, or definition on it). You look at the front side of the card. Your partner will say and spell the word in English. If your partner makes a mistake, correct him or her. Then your partner will do the same with one of your cards. Continue until you review all of the cards.

C. Go back to the vocabulary list at the beginning of each chapter. What did you learn about the target words? Add your numbers to the lists.

Vocabulary Practice 1, see page 193

Telling Stories

▶ THINK BEFORE YOU READ

A. Work with a partner. Look at the picture. Ask and answer the questions. If you don't know a word in English, ask your partner or look in your dictionary. Then write your new words on page 191.

    1. What animal do you see?

    2. What is it doing?

B. Work with a partner. Ask and answer the questions.

    1. In what kind of book would you find the picture above?

    2. Are there a lot of these kinds of stories in your culture?

    3. Do you enjoy these kinds of stories? Why or why not?

Folktales

> PREPARE TO READ

A. Look at the words (and phrases) in the list. Write the number(s) next to each word to show what you know. You may be able to write more than one number next to some of the words. You will study all of these words in this chapter.

   1. I can use the word in a sentence.

   2. I know <u>one meaning</u> of the word.

   3. I know <u>more than one meaning</u> of the word.

   4. I know how to pronounce the word.

B. Work with a partner. Look at the picture. Ask and answer the questions. If you don't know a word in English, ask your partner or look in your dictionary. Then write your new words on page 191.

   1. What are the names in English for the two insects?

   2. What is happening? What are the insects doing?

   3. What is the story behind the picture? If you know it, tell it to your partner.

_____ behavior

_____ characteristic

_____ clever

_____ grass

_____ lie

_____ meal

_____ punish

_____ share

_____ the same

_____ trick

Reading Skill: Understanding Topics

The main topic of a reading answers the question "What is the reading about?" The title often tells you the topic. Sometimes there are *headings* for different parts of the reading. The headings divide the reading into smaller topics. The smaller topics, called *subtopics*, support the main topic. When you preview a text, always look for headings.

C. Preview the reading "Folktales." Then answer the questions.

1. What is the title of the story that goes with the picture on page 15?

2. What is the main topic of the reading?

3. What are the subtopics?

> READ

Read "Folktales." Underline your answers to the questions for Exercise C.

⚘ Folktales ⚘

The Ant and the Grasshopper

1   One sunny winter day, an ant is eating in the sun. A hungry grasshopper is walking by. He asks the ant if he can **share** his **meal**.

"Why do you ask me for food? What were you doing in the summer?" asks the
5   ant.

"Oh," answers the grasshopper, "I was singing all summer."

"Well then," says the ant, "you sang all summer, you can dance all winter."

"The Ant and the Grasshopper" is a *folktale*. Folktales are very old stories. They usually explain something about human **behavior** or the natural world. Folktales
10   were not written down. Parents told them to their children, and their children told them to their children, and so on.

Every culture has folktales. The stories are different, but the ideas are often **the same**. There are many different kinds of folktales. Often one story has **characteristics** of more than one kind. Here are four kinds of folktales.

15   *Fables*

In a fable, the characters are animals, but they behave like humans. A fable always teaches something. This is called the *moral*. Sometimes the moral is told at the end of the story. Other times the listener has to think about it. "The Ant and the Grasshopper" is a fable.

20 *Pourquoi Stories*
    Pourquoi means *why* in French. Pourquoi stories explain something about the natural world. For example, a story might answer the question, "Why is the **grass** green?"

Trickster Tales
25   A *trickster* is a **clever** character who **lies** and plays **tricks** on other characters. Tricksters are often animals. Usually, no one **punishes** them for their bad behavior.

Fairy Tales
    A fairy tale has one or more characters with magical[1] power. There are good
30 characters and bad characters. The bad characters are usually punished, and most stories end happily.

---

[1] **magical:** having a special power that makes impossible things happen

Vocabulary Check

Complete the sentences with the boldfaced words from the reading.

1. In English, the morning _____ is called breakfast.

2. April 1 is called April Fool's Day. On that day, children play

_____ on each other.

3. He's a _____ little boy. He always has the correct answer.

4. We have _____ birthday. We both were born on August 30.

5. The _____ is green now because of the rain.

6. He always tells the truth. He never _____.

7. That child never listens to me, and he lies all the time. I'm going to tell his

mother about his bad _____.

8. I'll _____ my lunch with you if you show me your

homework.

9. One of the _____ of a fable is that it always teaches

something.

10. My little brother kicks me all the time, but my mother never

_____ him. She says he's just a baby.

READ AGAIN

Read "Folktales" again and complete the comprehension exercises. As you work, keep the reading goal in mind.

> **READING GOAL:** To understand the characteristics of four different kinds of folktales

Comprehension Check

A. Complete the chart. Check (✓) the characteristics of the different types of folktales.

Characteristic	Fable	Pourquoi story	Trickster tale	Fairy tale
1. magical powers				
2. a clever character				
3. animals behave like humans				
4. the main character lies				
5. usually has a happy ending				
6. a moral at the end				
7. explains something about the natural world				
8. punishment for bad behavior				

B. Think of a folktale to tell your classmates. Draw pictures on a separate sheet of paper to help you remember the story. Look up any words you need and write them under the pictures. Look at the words and pictures and practice telling your story.

C. Work in small groups. Tell your folktales. Check (✓) the characteristics in the chart for each folktale. Then write what kind of folktale you think it is. Remember, some stories have characteristics of more than one kind of folktale.

Characteristic	Student 1	Student 2	Student 3	Student 4
magical powers				
a clever character				
animals behave like humans				
the main character lies				
usually has a happy ending				
a moral at the end				
explains something about the natural world				
punishment for bad behavior				
What kind of folktale is it?				

> DISCUSS

Work in small groups. Ask and answer the questions.

1. What is the moral of "The Ant and the Grasshopper"? Explain your answer. (There is more than one correct answer.)

2. In your culture, do you have a story with a similar moral? What is the story? Tell it to your group.

Vocabulary Skill: Adjectives

Adjectives are words that describe nouns (people, places, things, or ideas). Adjectives come in front of the nouns that they describe. They can also come after a linking verb such as *be, feel, seem, look, taste,* or *smell*.

EXAMPLES:

a *safe* city
a *flat* table
a *clever* idea
He looks *relaxed*.

A. Read the sentences. Underline the adjectives.

1. You are a very <u>clever</u> boy.

2. There are no waves today. The surface of the water is flat.

3. His legs are powerful.

4. After I exercise, I always feel relaxed.

5. I like natural food.

6. My mother cooked a special meal for my birthday.

B. Work in small groups. Ask and answer the questions. Use the boldfaced adjectives in your answers.

1. When do you feel **relaxed**?

2. Do you have any **natural** abilities, such as a **natural** ability in music, dance, math, art, or a sport?

3. Is your city **safe**?

4. Are your feet **flat**?

5. Who is the **clever**est person you know?

Anansi and Turtle

> PREPARE TO READ

A. Look at the words (and phrases) in the list. Write the number(s) next to each word to show what you know. You may be able to write more than one number next to some of the words. You will study all of these words in this chapter.

1. I can use the word in a sentence.

2. I know <u>one meaning</u> of the word.

3. I know <u>more than one meaning</u> of the word.

4. I know how to pronounce the word.

B. Work with a partner. Look at the picture. Ask and answer the questions. If you don't know a word in English, ask your partner or look in your dictionary. Then write your new words on page 191.

1. What animals do you see?

2. Where are they?

3. What is happening?

_____ apologize

_____ ashamed

_____ as soon as

_____ bottom

_____ covered

_____ dirty

_____ follow

_____ pocket

_____ remove

_____ shoulder

C. Read the first three paragraphs of the story "Anansi and Turtle." Circle the sequence words. Then put the sentences in order. Write *1* next to the first thing that happened, *2* next to the second, and so on.

_____ Anansi invited Turtle to dinner.

_____ Anansi told Turtle that his hands were dirty.

_____ Turtle walked by and smelled the food.

_____ Anansi was eating dinner.

_____ Turtle sat down.

> READ

Read "Anansi and Turtle." Circle the sequence words.

ೲ Anansi and Turtle ೲ

1   Anansi the spider was eating his evening meal when his friend Turtle walked by. "Hello, Anansi," said Turtle. "That smells great!"
      Anansi loved to eat, and he didn't like to share. But in spider culture, you always share your food with a friend. So Anansi said, "Come in, Turtle, and eat
5   with me."
      Turtle sat down with a smile, but before Turtle could start eating, Anansi said, "Turtle, your hands are **dirty**! In my culture we wash our hands before we eat."
      Turtle looked at his dirty hands and felt **ashamed**. He **apologized** to Anansi and went to the river to wash. When he got back, Anansi was already eating.
10   "I didn't want the food to get cold," Anansi explained.
      Turtle sat down at the table. Now he was really hungry, but Anansi said, "Turtle, your hands are still dirty!"
      Turtle looked down. Anansi was right! "I'm so sorry! I don't know what happened. I'll wash them again," Turtle said.
15   This time, Turtle walked back from the river on the grass. His hands were clean when he got to the table. But to his surprise, all of the food was gone! "I'm sorry, Turtle, but you took so long! I couldn't wait," Anansi explained.
      The next day Turtle was swimming in the river when he saw Anansi. "Hello, Anansi, would you like to have lunch with me?"
20   "Oh, yes!" said Anansi.
      "Then **follow** me!" said Turtle.

Turtle and Anansi swam to the **bottom** of the river. There, Anansi saw a table **covered** with food. He was very hungry, but there was a problem. Every time he tried to sit down, he popped[1] back up to the surface of the river.

25   Then Anansi had a clever idea. He put some rocks[2] in his jacket **pockets** and swam back down to the bottom of the river. He sat down at the table and smiled. But before he could eat anything, Turtle said, "In my culture, we **remove** our jackets at the table."

Anansi saw that Turtle wasn't wearing a jacket, and he felt ashamed. But **as** 30   **soon as** his jacket was off his **shoulders**, he popped back up to the surface again. On the river bottom below, clever Turtle smiled and started eating.

---

[1] **pop up:** move quickly and suddenly from the bottom of something to the top

[2] **rock:** stone that forms part of the Earth's surface

Vocabulary Check

Look at the pictures and read the definitions on the next page. Write the target word from the list on page 21 next to the correct picture or definition.

1. _____ =

2. _____ =

3. _____ =

top

4. _____ =

(continued on next page)

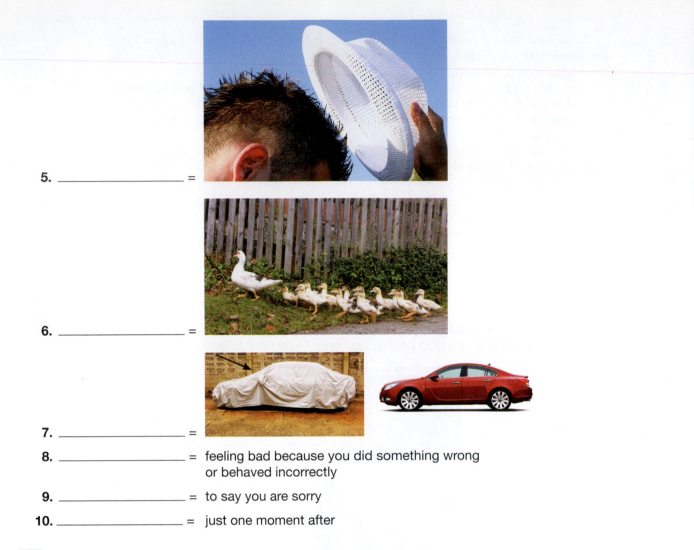

5. _____ =

6. _____ =

7. _____ =

8. _____ = feeling bad because you did something wrong or behaved incorrectly

9. _____ = to say you are sorry

10. _____ = just one moment after

> READ AGAIN

Read "Anansi and Turtle" again and complete the comprehension exercises on the next page. As you work, keep the reading goal in mind.

> 📖 **READING GOAL:** To identify the moral of "Anansi and Turtle"

Comprehension Check

A. Complete the summary of "Anansi and Turtle." Use the words in the list. Be sure to capitalize the first letter of the first word in a sentence.

ashamed	clean	grass	remove
as soon as	dirty	meal	~~share~~
bottom	followed	pockets	surface

Part 1

Anansi didn't want to (1)_____ *share* _____ his (2)_____ with Turtle. He told Turtle that his hands were (3)_____. Turtle felt (4)_____. When Turtle went to wash his hands, Anansi started eating. When Turtle got back to the table, Anansi told him that his hands still weren't (5)_____. Turtle washed his hands in the river again and walked back on the (6)_____. His hands were clean, but there wasn't any food. Anansi had eaten it all.

Part 2

Anansi (7)_____ Turtle to the (8)_____ of the river. Anansi tried to sit at the table, but he popped back up to the (9)_____. Then he put some rocks in his (10)_____. He swam down to the table and sat down. Turtle asked him to (11)_____ his jacket. (12)_____ he did, he popped back up to the surface.

B. Put the events from the **first part of the story** into the correct sequence. Write *1* next to the first event, *2* next to the second, and so on.

_____ There was no more food because Anansi had eaten it all.

_____ Turtle sat down to eat, but Anansi told him that his hands were dirty.

_____ Turtle washed his hands again and walked back on the grass.

_____ Turtle washed his hands at the river, but they got dirty again.

_____ Anansi invited Turtle to share his meal.

C. Put the events from the **second part of the story** into the correct sequence. Write *1* next to the first event, *2* next to the second, and so on.

_____ As soon as Anansi removed his jacket, he popped back up to the surface.

_____ Anansi put rocks in his jacket pockets.

_____ Anansi sat down to eat with his jacket on, but Turtle asked him to remove it.

_____ Turtle started eating.

_____ Turtle invited Anansi to lunch.

_____ Anansi tried to sit down, but he popped back up to the surface.

D. What do you think the moral of "Anansi and Turtle" is? Write it here. Then share your moral with the class. (There are many possible answers.)

_____

> DISCUSS

Work in small groups. Ask and answer the questions.

1. In your opinion, who wrote the best moral (Exercise D above)? Why do you think it is the best? Do you have a story with the same moral in your culture? What is it?

2. Talk about a time when you felt ashamed because you didn't know the correct way to behave.

Learn the Vocabulary

A. Add an example sentence to the back of each of the cards that you made for Unit 1.

B. Make cards for the words from Unit 2 that were new to you when you started the unit. Include target words and words that you wrote on page 191. Write an example sentence for each word.

C. Work with a partner. Quiz each other on all of your cards (Units 1 and 2). If you can't remember a word, your partner will read the example sentence on the card but will say "blank" in place of the word. If you still can't remember the word, your partner will put that card to one side. Then have your partner quiz you on that card again after you finish all of your other cards.

EXAMPLE:

Student A: In a trickster tale, no one "blank" a character for bad behavior.

Student B: Punishes!

Student A: Yes. That's correct.

D. Go back to the vocabulary list at the beginning of each chapter. What did you learn about the target words? Add your numbers to the list.

Vocabulary Practice 2, see page 194

> THINK BEFORE YOU READ

A. Work with a partner. Look at the picture. What kinds of food do you see? Label the picture. If you don't know a word in English, ask your partner or look in your dictionary. Then write your new words on page 191.

B. Work with a partner. Ask and answer the questions.

1. Which of the foods in the picture do you like? Which don't you like?

2. The title of Chapter 5 is "Dangerous Dining." What kinds of food can be dangerous?

3. The title of Chapter 6 is "Wild Treasures." Look up the words "wild" and "treasure" in your dictionary. What kinds of food might be called a *wild treasure*?

Dangerous Dining

> PREPARE TO READ

A. Look at the words in the list. Write the number(s) next to each word to show what you know. You may be able to write more than one number next to some of the words. You will study all of these words in this chapter.

1. I can use the word in a sentence.

2. I know <u>one meaning</u> of the word.

3. I know <u>more than one meaning</u> of the word.

4. I know how to pronounce the word.

B. Work with a partner. Look at the picture. Ask and answer the questions. If you don't know a word in English, ask your partner or look in your dictionary. Then write your new words on page 191.

1. Do you know the name of the fish in the picture? Have you ever eaten it?

2. Did you ever eat something that made you sick? Tell your partner.

_____ dangerous

_____ death

_____ license

_____ pass

_____ poisonous

_____ practical

_____ prepare

_____ raw

_____ responsible

_____ survive

You *scan* a text to look for specific information. When you scan, you do not read all the words. You move your eyes very quickly over the words, and you stop when you find the information you need.

C. Scan the Web article "Dangerous Dining" on the next page. Then complete the chart. If you can't find the answer to a question, write the link that you should click on to find the answer. The links are underlined in blue on the Web page.

Question	Answer	Link
1. In which part of the world do people eat fugu?	*Japan*	
2. What are two other names for *fugu*?		
3. How many people die after eating fugu every year?		
4. Which important people died after eating fugu?	*?*	*people die from fugu poisoning*
5. Can you buy fugu in a supermarket to cook at home?		
6. When is the best time of year to eat fugu?		
7. What is the best fugu restaurant in Japan?		

READ

Read "Dangerous Dining." Were your answers for Exercise C correct?

---

http://www.dangerousdining.com

DANGEROUS DINING

1 *Fugu* is the Japanese word for puffer fish. It is also called Japanese blowfish. Fugu is the most **poisonous** fish in the world. Just a small taste of the deadly[1] poison can kill
5 you. But in Japan and other countries in the Far East, people pay hundreds of dollars to eat fugu. It will be the last meal for some of them. Why do people eat something so **dangerous**? Some people say they like
10 the taste. Others like to eat it *because* of the danger.

When chefs[2] **prepare** fugu, they first need to remove the poison from its body. They train for years to learn how to do that. At the end
15 of the training, they have to prepare their own fugu. To **pass** the test, they need to eat it—and **survive.**

MORE FACTS ABOUT FUGU

Fugu Deaths
20 Every year, about fifty people die from fugu poisoning. The deadliest year was 1958.

One hundred seventy-six people died. These days, however, fugu chefs are very well trained. You can feel safe eating fugu
25 prepared by a chef. Untrained home cooks are **responsible** for the small number of **deaths** every year.

Fugu Chefs
Fugu chefs need a **license** to prepare fugu.
30 All fugu restaurants must put the chef's license in the window. To get a fugu license, you must train with a licensed fugu chef. The training can take years. Then you must **pass** a written and **practical** examination. For the
35 practical exam, you have twenty minutes to prepare and eat the fish. Only about 30 percent pass the practical exam.

Eating Fugu
Winter is the best time to eat fugu. That is
40 when the fish are fat and not as poisonous. A fugu meal can be very expensive. **Raw** fugu, called *fugu sashimi,* can cost as much as $200 per person.

---

[1] **deadly:** able to kill you

[2] **chef:** someone whose job is cooking in a restaurant

Vocabulary Check

Circle the letter of the correct answer to complete each sentence. The boldfaced words are the target words.

1. In most countries, you need a **license** to _____.
   a. cook   **b.** drive   **c.** eat

2. Sit down and I'll **prepare** a _____ for you.
   a. cookie   **b.** glass of milk   **c.** sandwich

3. Every year, there are many **deaths** from _____.
   a. car accidents   **b.** hospitals   **c.** examinations

4. I **passed** the test because I _____.
   a. forgot the answers   **b.** studied   **c.** was late

5. He is very _____. He probably won't **survive**.
   a. clever   **b.** relaxed   **c.** sick

6. It is **dangerous** to talk on your cell phone when you are _____.
   a. driving   **b.** eating   **c.** relaxing

7. Chocolate is **poisonous** to most dogs. It can _____ them.
   a. follow   **b.** kill   **c.** punish

8. Teachers need to go to college, but they also need **practical** training in the _____.
   a. classroom   **b.** gym   **c.** home

9. You are **responsible** for the safety of your little brother. If he gets hurt, _____ will be punished.
   a. he   **b.** we   **c.** you

10. The Japanese sometimes _____ fish, but they often eat it **raw**.
   a. buy   **b.** cook   **c.** eat

> READ AGAIN

Read "Dangerous Dining" again and complete the comprehension exercises on the next page. As you work, keep the reading goal in mind.

> 📖 **READING GOAL:** To remember some interesting facts about fugu

Comprehension Check

A. Answer the questions. Try not to look back at the reading.

1. Why is it dangerous to eat fugu?

   _____

2. Why do people like to eat fugu?

   _____

3. What do you need to do to become a fugu chef in Japan?

   _____

4. Who is responsible for most of the deaths from fugu these days?

   _____

5. Why is it best to eat fugu in the winter?

   _____

B. There are seven mistakes (including the example) in the summary of "Dangerous Dining." Find the mistakes and correct them. Try not to look back at the reading.

     poisonous
Fugu is the most ~~interesting~~ fish in the world. You need to remove the

body before you eat it. In Japan, chefs who want to cook fugu train for

weeks. Then they take a test. The test has two parts: one written and one

practical. To pass the written test, they need to prepare and eat poison

and survive. About 70 percent of them pass the test and get their licenses

as fugu chefs. These days, eating at a fugu restaurant is very dangerous.

Almost all fugu deaths happen when people prepare and eat fugu at home.

C. Now look back at the reading. Check your answers for Exercise B. Correct any mistakes.

> DISCUSS

Work in small groups. Ask and answer the questions.

1. Why do you think some people like to eat things that are dangerous?
2. Do you like to try food that you have never tasted before? Why or why not?
3. What is the most unusual thing you have ever eaten?

Wild Treasures

PREPARE TO READ

A. Look at the words (and phrases) in the list. Write the number(s) next to each word to show what you know. You may be able to write more than one number next to some of the words. You will study all of these words in this chapter.

1. I can use the word in a sentence.

2. I know <u>one meaning</u> of the word.

3. I know <u>more than one meaning</u> of the word.

4. I know how to pronounce the word.

B. Work with a partner. Look at the picture. Ask and answer the questions. If you don't know a word in English, ask your partner or look in your dictionary. Then write your new words on page 191.

1. Where are the man and the dog?

2. What are they doing?

3. What is the dog smelling?

_____ agree

_____ full

_____ ground

_____ imagine

_____ in fact

_____ joke

_____ luck

_____ scientist

_____ serious

_____ wild

Reading Skill: Understanding Details

Details are specific pieces of information. They support the main topic and the subtopics of a reading. They help you understand the main ideas in a reading.

C. Read the questions. Then read the first paragraph of the newspaper article "Wild Treasures" to find the answers. As you work, try to guess what "it" means.

1. What does it smell like?
2. Who likes to eat it?
3. What does it taste like?
4. Where can you find it?
5. How much does it cost?
6. What is **it**?

 **READ**

Read "Wild Treasures." Did you guess what **it** is?

Wild Treasures

1　　It smells like rotten[1] eggs. Pigs love it. Great chefs do, too. The best way to prepare it? Raw, cut very thin, on top of pasta. (The pigs don't **agree** about the pasta.) The taste? **Imagine**
5　the smell of dark, black, rich dirt. Then add the taste of fine wine and very strong cheese. Where can you get it? With a lot of **luck**, a well-trained dog, and a plane ticket to Italy, you **might** find it under a tree. The price? From
10　$1,200 to $2,300 a pound ($2,600 to $5,000 a kilogram).

　　The white truffle is the king[2] of the mushroom world. **In fact**, it is the second most expensive food in the world. (The first is
15　caviar.[3]) Most of these very special mushrooms grow in Italy. You cannot grow them in your vegetable garden. They are found only in the **wild**. They grow under the **ground** at the bottom of oak and hazelnut[4] trees. Dogs and
20　pigs, with their excellent noses, are very good at finding them. But pigs love the taste of truffles a little too much, so these days most truffle hunters use dogs.

　　Giovanni Monchiero is a truffle hunter.[5] He
25　also trains truffle-hunting dogs at the University of Truffle Hunting Dogs in a small town in Italy. No, that's not a **joke**. Truffle hunting is a **serious**, sometimes dangerous, business in Italy. In fact, well-trained truffle dogs are sometimes
30　kidnapped[6] or poisoned.

　　Most truffle hunters start at a very young age, usually when they are children. Truffle hunters don't talk about their work very much. They don't want others to know where they find
35　their truffles. Isabelle Gianicolo is a **scientist** who studies the mushrooms. She says it is very difficult to get any information from truffle hunters. "They have pockets **full** of truffles. They smell like a truffle … " says Gianicolo.
40　But they lie and say, "No, I don't have any!"

---

[1] **rotten:** bad and soft because old or wet

[2] **king:** the most important member of a group

[3] **caviar:** a special, very expensive type of fish eggs

[4] **hazelnut:** a sweet, round nut

[5] **hunter:** a person or animal who looks for someone or something very carefully

[6] **kidnap:** take a person or an animal away illegally and possibly demand money for returning him/her/it

Vocabulary Check

Complete the sentences with the boldfaced words from the reading.

1. In the springtime, the _____ is covered with grass.

2. The swimming pool is _____ of water.

3. A(n) _____ has many years of special training in some field of science, such as biology or chemistry.

4. Everyone was laughing at the _____ he told.

5. I think animals such as elephants, lions, and tigers should live in the _____. I don't think zoos are good places for them.

6. Close your eyes and _____ that you are on a beautiful beach.

7. Stop laughing. I'm not joking. This is a very _____ problem.

8. My friend thinks that fish tastes good, but I don't _____. I don't like the taste.

9. Fugu is poisonous. _____, it is the most poisonous fish in the world.

10. I have very bad _____. I never win anything.

> READ AGAIN

Read "Wild Treasures" again and complete the comprehension exercises on the next page. As you work, keep the reading goal in mind.

> READING GOAL: To remember some details about white truffles

Comprehension Check

A. Circle the letter of the correct answer(s) to complete each sentence. (Some sentences have more than one correct answer.)

1. _____ are very good at finding truffles.
   a. Great chefs
   b. Trained dogs
   c. Pigs

2. Most truffle hunters use trained dogs, not pigs, because _____.
   a. pigs can't smell very well
   b. pigs like to eat the truffles they find
   c. dogs love to eat truffles

3. The most expensive white truffles cost _____.
   a. more than caviar
   b. $5,000 a kilogram
   c. $1,200 a pound

4. Truffle hunting is a serious business because _____.
   a. truffles are very difficult to find
   b. people pay very high prices for truffles
   c. many people get hurt in the wild

5. Giovanni Monchiero _____.
   a. trains dogs to hunt for truffles
   b. poisons truffle hunting dogs
   c. is a truffle hunter

6. Most truffle hunters _____.
   a. start their training when they are children
   b. tell others where to find the best truffles
   c. want to help scientists who study mushrooms

B. Work with a partner. Take turns asking and answering the questions. Try not to look back at the reading.

1. What do white truffles taste like? What do they smell like?

2. Where do they grow? How can you find them?

3. How do chefs prepare them?

4. How much do they cost?

5. Why don't truffle hunters like to talk about their work?

C. Now look back at the reading. Check your answers for Exercise B. How many answers did you remember correctly? _____

> DISCUSS

Work in small groups. Ask and answer the questions.

1. Why do you think someone would poison a truffle dog? Why would someone kidnap a truffle dog?

2. Do a lot of people in your country like to pick and eat wild mushrooms?

3. Have you ever picked or eaten wild mushrooms?

4. Fugu and white truffles are very expensive. What are some other expensive foods?

> VOCABULARY SKILL BUILDING

Vocabulary Skill: Word Families

Many words in English belong to word families. In one word family, there can be several forms of a word. Words in the same word family have the same base, or main part, but different endings, called *suffixes*. The suffix often changes the part of speech (noun, verb, adjective, adverb), but it does not change the central meaning of the word.

EXAMPLE:

imagine (verb)   *imagination* (noun)   *imaginary* (adjective)

A. Look at the words that are in the same families as some of the target words from Chapters 1–6. Complete the chart with the target words.

Noun	Adjective
danger	
nature	
poison	
responsibility	
safety	
seriousness	
specialist	
	energetic
	lucky
	powerful

B. Complete the sentences with the noun or adjective form of the words in the chart. Be careful. You will use only one form of each word.

1. Your medical problem is unusual. You need to see a(n)

   _____.

2. The police are responsible for the _____ of everyone in

   the city.

3. Good swimmers usually have _____ arms and legs.

4. We are in _____ ! Quick, call the police.

5. Babies can't talk, so they cry when they are hungry. It is

   _____ for babies to cry. It is not unusual.

6. Here, let me pick the numbers. I usually have good _____.

7. I don't have much _____ today. I think I'm getting sick.

8. She died because she drank _____.

9. I'm _____. I'm not joking.

10. Your teacher can help you, but your learning is your own

    _____.

Learn the Vocabulary

A. Make cards for the words from Chapters 5 and 6 that were new to you when you started the unit. Include target words and words that you wrote on page 191.

B. Review your new cards one time with a partner. Then add your cards from Chapters 1–4 to the new cards and review all of them. As your partner quizzes you, he or she will put your cards in two groups: one group for the words you remembered, and one group for the words you didn't remember. Keep the two groups separate. Write the number of cards you remembered. _____

C. For the next three days, review the first group of cards (the ones you remembered) once a day. Review the second group of cards twice a day. Remember to change the order of the cards in each group before you review them. Each time you review your cards, make a check (✓) in the chart.

Day one	Day two	Day three
Group 1: _____	Group 1: _____	Group 1: _____
Group 2: _____, _____	Group 2: _____, _____	Group 2: _____, _____

D. After three days, put the two groups back together, change the order, and review all of the cards with your partner in class. How many words did you remember this time? _____

E. Go back to the vocabulary list at the beginning of each chapter. What did you learn about the target words? Add your numbers to the lists.

Vocabulary Practice 3, see page 195

FLUENCY PRACTICE 1

Fluency Strategy

To improve your reading speed and fluency, time yourself as you read something that is very easy for you. Then read it again. Push yourself to read it faster the second time.

Easy means:
- You know all or almost all of the words (98-100%).
- The sentences are easy to understand.
- You can read quickly and still understand.
- Reading feels natural and relaxed.

> READING 1

Before You Read

A. Read the definition for *wig*. You will see this word in the reading.

> **wig:** a cover for the head that looks like real hair, but is not

B. Preview "The Gift, Part 1" on the next page. What do you think it is about? Circle the letter of the correct answer.

   a. a lucky gift

   b. a gift of love

   c. a Christmas gift

Read

A. Read "The Gift, Part 1." Time yourself. Write your start and end times and your total reading time. Then calculate your reading speed (words per minute) and write it in the progress chart on page 205.

Start time: _____   **End time:** _____   **Total time:** _____ (in seconds)

Reading speed:
364 words ÷ _____ (total time in seconds) x 60 = _____ words per minute

❧ The Gift, Part 1 ❧

1   One dollar and eighty-seven cents. That is all. Three times Della counts it, but the number doesn't change: One dollar and eighty-seven cents. And the next day is Christmas. Della begins to cry.

     While Della cries, let's look around us. What do we see? The year is 1905, and
5   the month is December. The city is New York. The apartment is small and simple. It has only two rooms. Mr. and Mrs. James (Jim) Dillingham Young live here. It is their first home, and they pay $8 a week for it.

     Jim works six days a week for $20. At the end of every long day, he is tired and his feet hurt. But then he opens the door of the apartment, and there she is!
10   Mrs. Young, his wife, his Della! She looks at him with her brown eyes full of love, and Jim forgets the long day and the cold, dark walk home. He knows that he is a very lucky man.

     Jim and Della do not have very much, but they do have two special things. They are Della's hair, and Jim's gold watch. Della's beautiful hair covers her
15   shoulders. It falls in soft waves down her back.

     Their second special thing is Jim's watch. Jim's grandfather gave it to Jim's father, and Jim's father gave it to him. Sometimes Della and Jim play a little game. Della asks, "Excuse me, sir? Could you please tell me the time?" Then Jim smiles. He removes the gold watch from his pocket and tells Della the time. It is their
20   little joke.

     But now let's go back to Della. She is not crying anymore, but she is very serious. It is December 24th. She is looking at the money on the table, and she is thinking.

     "How can I buy a gift for Jim with $1.87? What am I going to do?"
25   Della looks out the window and sees herself in the glass. She sees her long hair and then looks at the money on the table. Suddenly, she has a clever idea. She puts on her thin black coat and old hat and runs to Mrs. Sofronie's wig store on First Street.

B. Read "The Gift, Part 1" again, a little faster this time. Write your start and end times and your total reading time. Then calculate your reading speed (words per minute) and write it in the progress chart on page 205.

Start time: _____   **End time:** _____   **Total time:** _____ (in seconds)

Reading speed:
364 words ÷ _____ (total time in seconds) x 60 = _____ words per minute

Comprehension Check

A. Circle the letter of the correct answer to complete each sentence.

1. Della _____.
   a. is Mrs. Young
   b. works in a wig store
   c. is Mrs. Sofronie

2. Jim does not _____.
   a. like his job
   b. love his wife
   c. like the apartment

3. Della wants to _____.
   a. buy Jim a new watch
   b. move to a bigger apartment
   c. buy Jim a Christmas gift

4. Della is going to _____.
   a. sell Jim's watch
   b. buy a wig
   c. sell her hair

B. Complete the summary of "The Gift, Part 1."

It is Christmas. Jim's life is not easy, but Della makes him

(1) _____. He loves her beautiful (2) _____.

Della wants to get a (3) _____ gift for Jim, but she

doesn't have much (4) _____. She decides to

(5) _____ her hair to Mrs. Sofronie. She will use the money to

(6) _____ something special for (7) _____.

C. Check your answers for the comprehension questions in the Answer Key on page 206. Then calculate your score and write it in the progress chart on page 205.

_____ (my number correct) ÷ 11 x 100 = _____%

> READING 2

Before You Read

What will happen in the final part of "The Gift"? Make two predictions.

1. _____

2. _____

Read

A. Read "The Gift, Part 2." Time yourself. Write your start and end times and your total reading time. Then calculate your reading speed (words per minute) and write it in the progress chart on page 205.

Start time: _____ **End time:** _____ **Total time:** _____ (in seconds)

Reading speed:

441 words ÷ _____ (total time in seconds) x 60 = _____ words per minute

---

৯০ The Gift, Part 2 ৫

1   Mrs. Sofronie buys hair and uses it to make wigs.
"How much will you pay me for my hair?" Della asks.
Mrs. Sofronie thinks for a minute. Della's hair is long and thick. Then she says,
"Twenty dollars."
5   "OK," Della agrees, "but please, do it quickly."
Mrs. Sofronie starts cutting. Della imagines the gift she will buy for Jim and
tries not to look at her hair on the floor. Mrs. Sofronie finishes and gives Della
$20. Della takes the money and runs to Fourth Street. After two hours, she finds
the perfect gift: a gold chain for Jim's watch. The price? $21.
10   Della runs home with the chain and 87 cents in her pocket. It is late, and she
needs to prepare the evening meal. Suddenly, she sees herself in the window. For
the first time, she sees her short hair and thinks, "Will Jim still love me?"
At seven o'clock, Della hears Jim at the door. He looks thin and cold. Her heart fills
with love for her husband. Then Jim sees Della's hair. He is very quiet, and he looks sad.
15   "Jim, talk to me! Please don't be sad. I have a special gift for you. Let's be
happy. It's Christmas tomorrow," Della says.
"But…," Jim says. "Where is your beautiful hair?"
"Oh Jim, I'm sorry," Della apologizes. "Mrs. Sofronie has my hair, but I have a
gift for you. And I love you," Della says.
20   Jim looks at Della for a minute. Then he says, "Della, I loved your long hair
because it was a part of you, and I love you with short hair. And I have a special
gift for you, too."
Della opens the gift. Inside, there are two very expensive hair combs. They
are beautiful, but she can't wear them. Her hair is too short. She looks up at Jim.
25   "They're beautiful," she says. Her eyes are full of tears, but she smiles and says,
"Here is my gift for you."
Jim opens his gift slowly. When he sees the gold chain, he cannot speak.
"Do you like it? Let's put it on your watch!" says Della.
But Jim sits down and says, "Della, let's put our gifts away."
30   Della doesn't understand. "What's wrong? Don't you like it?"
"Oh Della, I love it," Jim says, "but I don't have my watch anymore."
"But…" Della says. Then suddenly, she understands. She sold her one special
thing to buy Jim's gift. And he did the same. Della smiles through her tears, and
Jim smiles back.
35   So there it is—a simple story of two people. Two people with nothing, but who
have everything they need.

B. Read "The Gift, Part 2" again, a little faster this time. Write your start and end times and your total reading time. Then calculate your reading speed (words per minute) and write it in the progress chart on page 205.

Start time: _____   End time: _____   Total time: _____ (in seconds)

Reading speed:
441 words ÷ _____ (total time in seconds) x 60 = _____ words per minute

C. Check the predictions you made on page 43. Were they correct?

Comprehension Check

A. Complete the sentences. Circle the letter of the correct answer.

1. Della decides to sell her hair to Mrs. Sofronie because she wants _____.
   a. an expensive wig   **b.** money   **c.** short hair

2. Della doesn't look at her hair on the floor because _____.
   a. she liked her long hair   **b.** she wants short   **c.** her hair is dirty
                                          hair

3. With the money from her hair, Della buys a _____.
   a. meal   **b.** watch   **c.** gold chain

4. When Jim sees Della's short hair, he is _____.
   a. sad   **b.** angry   **c.** thin and cold

5. Jim _____ to buy Della's gift.
   a. sells his watch   **b.** asks his father   **c.** works hard
                                      for money

B. What is the moral of the story? Check (✓) the correct answer.

_____ **1.** The poor are often happier than the rich.

_____ **2.** Never sell the things that you love.

_____ **3.** Love is the best gift of all.

C. Check your answers for the comprehension questions in the Answer Key on page 206. Then calculate your score and write it in the progress chart on page 205.

_____ (my number correct) ÷ 6 x 100 = _____%

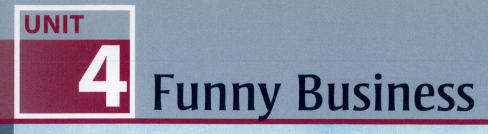

UNIT 4

Funny Business

> THINK BEFORE YOU READ

A. Work with a partner. Look at the cartoon. Ask and answer the questions. If you don't know a word in English, ask your partner or look in your dictionary. Then write your new words on page 191.

1. How many people are there in the cartoon?

2. What is happening?

3. The title of the cartoon is "Miscommunication." What does "Miscommunication" mean? Why is it a good title for this cartoon?

B. Work with a partner. Ask and answer the questions.

1. How often do you read cartoons or listen to jokes in your native language?

2. Do you ever read cartoons or listen to jokes in English? Are they easy or difficult for you to understand? Why?

3. Do you think that animals can laugh? Which animals?

The Science of Laughter

CHAPTER 7

> PREPARE TO READ

A. Look at the words (and phrases) in the list. Write the number(s) next to each word to show what you know. You may be able to write more than one number next to some of the words. You will study all of these words in this chapter.

1. I can use the word in a sentence.

2. I know <u>one meaning</u> of the word.

3. I know <u>more than one meaning</u> of the word.

4. I know how to pronounce the word.

B. Work with a partner. Look at the cartoon. Ask and answer the questions. If you don't know a word in English, ask your partner or look in your dictionary. Then write your new words on page 191.

1. What is happening in the cartoon?

2. Why are the rats laughing?

_____ active

_____ brain

_____ control

_____ emotion

_____ experiment

_____ find out

_____ fun

_____ popular

_____ similarity

_____ surprise

Good readers ask themselves questions as they read. Their minds are *active*. Here are some simple questions that you can ask as you read:
- What do I already know about this topic?
- What is new to me in this reading?
- What is interesting to me in this reading?

C. Preview the magazine article "The Science of Laughter." Then answer the questions.

1. What is the topic of the reading?

2. What do you already know about this topic?

3. What are two questions that you have about the topic?

> READ

Read "The Science of Laughter" and look for the answers to the questions for Exercise C, item 3. If you find an answer, underline it.

The Science of Laughter

1   We've all seen animals playing. But are they having **fun**? In the past, most scientists believed that only humans could have fun. But today, those beliefs are changing. More and
5   more scientists are studying animal **emotions** and play. And what they are **finding out** might **surprise** you.

For example, scientists have done **experiments** to show that some animals laugh.
10   They have learned that chimpanzees, dogs, and rats, among other animals, all laugh. Their laughs might not sound like human laughter, but they are laughing.

The idea of laughing chimpanzees and dogs
15   may not be difficult to imagine. We know that there are many **similarities** between humans and chimps. And anyone who has a dog knows that dogs like to play.

However, rats? Have you ever played with a
20   rat? Have you ever tickled[1] one? Scientists at a university in Ohio did. What happened? The rats laughed! Actually, they chirped,[2] which is the sound that rats make. And like humans, the rats chirped only when someone they knew and
25   liked tickled them.

But how do the scientists know that the rats were really laughing? They studied their **brains**. When humans laugh, one part of the brain is very **active**. When a rat chirps, that
30   part of its brain is active, too.

---

[1] **tickle:** move your fingers lightly over someone in order to make him/her laugh

[2] **chirp:** make a short high sound, like a bird

And scientists have found another interesting similarity between humans and rats. Rats like to be with the rats in their group who chirp the most. It seems that fun-loving 35 rats are **popular.**

Interesting, you might say, but is it really important? In fact, these kinds of experiments are teaching scientists a lot about the parts of the human brain that **control** emotions. 40 Someday, they hope to find out how to help unhappy people feel happier. And that's nothing to laugh at!

Vocabulary Check

Read the definitions. Write the target word from the list on page 47 next to the correct definition.

1. _____ enjoyment

2. _____ liked by others

3. _____ something that is almost the same but not exactly the same

4. _____ the part of the body that we use to think

5. _____ a strong feeling such as love or hate

6. _____ a scientific test to tell whether something is true or not

7. _____ to make someone or something do what you want or make something work in a particular way

8. _____ always doing things, or moving around a lot

9. _____ to make someone feel that something unexpected or unusual is happening

10. _____ to learn the truth about something

> READ AGAIN

Read "The Science of Laughter" again and complete the comprehension exercises on the next page. As you work, keep the reading goal in mind.

📖 **READING GOAL:** To tell a partner . . .

1. what you already knew before reading "The Science of Laughter."

2. what you learned.

3. what was interesting.

Comprehension Check

A. Circle the letter of the correct answer to complete each sentence. There is only one correct answer.

1. In the past, most scientists believed that _____.
    a. humans and animals had similar emotions
    b. animals did not have emotions
    c. animals did not know how to play

2. Scientists have done experiments to show that some animals _____.
    a. have fun
    b. laugh
    c. play

3. The writer is not surprised that _____.
    a. dogs and chimpanzees laugh
    b. all animals laugh
    c. rats laugh

4. In the experiment, the scientists studied the rats' brains while _____
    a. the scientists played
    b. the rats tickled each other
    c. the rats chirped

5. The scientists think that rat chirping is similar to human laughter because _____.
    a. the same parts of the brain are active
    b. the brain is active
    c. animal brains and human brains are the same

6. The rats chirped only when _____ tickled them.
    a. another rat
    b. a popular rat
    c. a person they knew and liked

7. Rats who chirp a lot are _____.
    a. similar to humans
    b. popular with other rats
    c. very surprising

8. These kinds of experiments _____.
    a. are funny but not very serious
    b. teach scientists about the human brain
    c. make people happy

B. Scan "The Science of Laughter" and follow the directions.

1. Underline the information you already knew before you read the text.

2. Circle the information that was new to you.

3. Put a box around the information that was interesting to you.

C. Work with a partner. Compare your answers for Exercise B.

> DISCUSS

Read the statements. Do you agree or disagree? Write a number for your opinion. Then talk in small groups. Explain your opinions.

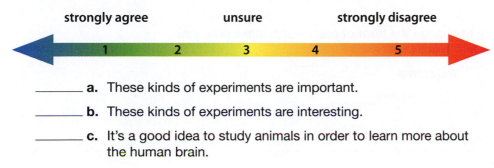

strongly agree   unsure   strongly disagree

1   2   3   4   5

_____ **a.** These kinds of experiments are important.

_____ **b.** These kinds of experiments are interesting.

_____ **c.** It's a good idea to study animals in order to learn more about the human brain.

_____ **d.** Playing with animals is fun.

> VOCABULARY SKILL BUILDING

Vocabulary Skill: The Suffixes -al and -ity

Adding a suffix to a word often changes its word form. For example, you can add the suffix -al to some nouns to make them adjectives. You can add the suffix -ity to some adjectives to make them nouns. If the word ends in -e, remove the -e before adding the suffix.

EXAMPLE:

nature (noun) + *-al* = *natural* (adjective)

active (adjective) + *-ity* = *activity* (noun)

A. Add the suffix *-al* or *-ity* to change the form of each word. Make sure you spell the new word forms correctly.

Noun	Adjective
1. nature	*natural*
2. behavior	_____
3. emotion	_____
4. experiment	_____
5. _____*activity*_____	active
6. _____	popular
7. practice	_____
8. _____	similar

B. Complete the sentences with the words from Exercise A. Use the correct word form (noun or adjective). You will use only one form of each word.

1. She's very _____. She laughs a lot, but she also cries a lot.

2. He has cancer. He is taking a(n) _____ drug. The doctors aren't sure whether it will help him or not.

3. I love everything about _____—the ocean, the mountains, the rivers!

4. You need a lot of _____ to play the piano well.

5. They are sisters. That is why they are so _____.

6. Young children do not like to sit all day. They like to move around and be _____.

Can't Take a Joke

> PREPARE TO READ

A. Look at the words (and phrases) in the list. Write the number(s) next to each word to show what you know. You may be able to write more than one number next to some of the words. You will study all of these words in this chapter.

1. I can use the word in a sentence.

2. I know <u>one meaning</u> of the word.

3. I know <u>more than one meaning</u> of the word.

4. I know how to pronounce the word.

B. Work with a partner. Look at the cartoon. Ask and answer the questions. If you don't know a word in English, ask your partner or look in your dictionary. Then write your new words on page 191.

1. Where are the people in the picture?

2. What is the man in the suit doing?

3. Why are the people laughing?

4. Why does the man in the suit think they are laughing?

_____ humorous

_____ interpreter

_____ introduction

_____ make fun of

_____ mistake

_____ offensive

_____ physical

_____ speech

_____ translate

C. Preview the magazine article "Can't Take a Joke." Then circle the letter of the correct answer to each question.

1. What is the main topic?
   a. speeches **b.** interpreters **c.** jokes **d.** culture

2. What is the main idea?
   a. Be careful when you tell a joke to someone from a different culture.
   b. Never start a speech with a joke.
   c. People from every culture like to have fun.
   d. Interpreters should not translate jokes.

> READ

Read "Can't Take a Joke" and think about the main idea you chose. At the end of each paragraph, decide if you chose the right main idea.

Can't Take a Joke

1 Imagine this situation: An American businessman is giving a **speech** in Germany. He doesn't speak German, so he is using an **interpreter**. In the **introduction** to
5 his speech, he tells a little joke. Everyone laughs. He's happy. His joke worked, right?
    Not so fast. In fact, they never heard his joke. The interpreter did not **translate** it. Why not? He knew that the joke was
10 **offensive** in German culture. So why did

everyone laugh? The interpreter told them to. He said, "The speaker has just told a joke. Please laugh."

Most interpreters would have done the
15 same thing. That's because jokes do not translate well from one culture to another. Different cultures find different things **humorous**. For example, Americans often **make fun of** themselves or others in their
20 jokes. But people from China, Japan, and other cultures in the Far East do not find that kind of joke funny. They don't think it is humorous to laugh at their own or other people's **mistakes**. Even worse, they might
25 feel offended by such a joke. That's why

we should be careful about using humor in cross-cultural[1] situations.

But isn't there even one joke that can make people from any culture laugh?
30 Probably not. However, there are similarities in what makes jokes funny. A good joke in any culture ends in a surprising way. You cannot imagine the ending. It is the surprise that makes us laugh.
35 **Physical** humor also works in every culture. That's why clowns[2] are popular all over the world. They use their bodies, not their words, to make people laugh. People from all cultures seem to enjoy that kind
40 of humor.

---

[1] **cross-cultural:** belonging to two or more societies, countries, or cultures
[2] **clown:** a person who wears makeup and funny clothes and tries to make people laugh

Vocabulary Check

Complete the sentences with the boldfaced words from the reading.

1. He told a very _____ story. I laughed a lot.

2. It is not nice to _____ other people. It makes them feel bad.

3. I made three serious _____, so I didn't pass the exam.

4. He can't control his legs. He has a(n) _____ problem.

5. He speaks five languages. He works as a(n) _____ at the United Nations.

6. This letter is in Spanish. I can't read it. Can you _____ it?

7. The scientist gave a(n) _____ about animal emotions. It was very long but interesting. Everyone listened carefully.

8. Your behavior was _____. You need to apologize.

9. The first paragraph of a reading is the _____. It starts the reading.

> READ AGAIN

Read "Can't Take a Joke" again and complete the comprehension exercises. As you work, keep the reading goal in mind.

> 📖 **READING GOAL:** To explain how humor can be dangerous in certain situations

Comprehension Check

A. Answer the questions. Write the paragraph numbers.

1. Which paragraphs talk about the dangers of humor? _____

2. Which paragraphs talk about similarities in humor in all cultures? _____

B. Check (✓) the true statements.

_____ 1. A businessman told a joke in a foreign country.

_____ 2. The people thought his joke was offensive.

_____ 3. The businessman didn't know that his joke was offensive.

_____ 4. Interpreters do not always translate jokes.

_____ 5. Making fun of people is a part of some cultures' humor.

_____ 6. There are many jokes that people from all cultures enjoy.

_____ 7. There are no similarities in the humor in different cultures.

_____ 8. Surprise endings and physical humor make most people laugh.

C. Work with a partner. Explain this sentence: *Humor can be dangerous.* Give a specific example, either from the article or from your personal experience. Do not look back at the article.

> DISCUSS

Work in small groups. Ask and answer the questions.

1. Name a movie or TV show that you think is funny. (It can be in any language.) What is funny about it?

2. In your culture, do people often laugh or make jokes about their own mistakes? Do you often make fun of yourself?

Learn the Vocabulary

A. Look at the dictionary page. What are the arrows (→) pointing at? Read the descriptions. Then write the letter in the space next to the arrow.

a. the division of syllables

b. how to pronounce the word

c. the syllable with stress

d. the part of speech (noun, verb, etc.)

e. the most common meaning of the word

f. a sentence using the word

g. a word that is often used with the word

h. words in the same word family

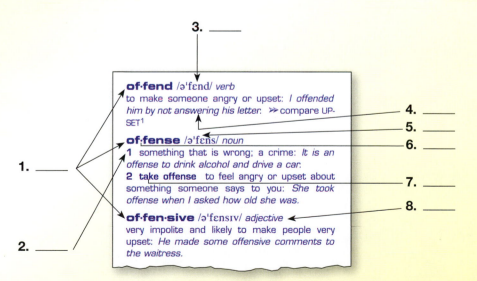

3. _____

of·fend /əˈfɛnd/ *verb*
to make someone angry or upset: *I offended him by not answering his letter.* ≫ compare UP-SET¹

4. _____
5. _____

of·fense /əˈfɛns/ *noun*
1 something that is wrong; a crime: *It is an offense to drink alcohol and drive a car.*
2 take offense to feel angry or upset about something someone says to you: *She took offense when I asked how old she was.*

6. _____

1. _____

7. _____

of·fen·sive /əˈfɛnsɪv/ *adjective*
very impolite and likely to make people very upset: *He made some offensive comments to the waitress.*

8. _____

2. _____

B. Look up the boldfaced words in a dictionary. Answer the questions.

  1. What part of speech is **humorous**? _____

  2. What other words are in the same family as **interpreter**? _____

  3. How many meanings are there for the noun **introduction**? _____

  4. What verb is often used in front of the noun **mistake**? _____

  5. How many example sentences are there for the adjective **active**? _____

C. Make cards for the words that were new to you in Chapters 7 and 8. Include target words and words that you wrote on page 191. Look up the words in a dictionary and find an example sentence for each word. Copy the sentence on the back of the word card.

D. Work with a partner. Quiz each other on all of your cards (Units 1–4). (See pages 13 and 27 for explanations of ways to quiz each other.)

E. Go back to the vocabulary list at the beginning of each chapter. What did you learn about the target words? Add your numbers to the lists.

Vocabulary Practice 4, see page 196

Some of My Best Friends Are Animals

▶ THINK BEFORE YOU READ

A. Work with a partner. Look at the picture. Ask and answer the questions. If you don't know a word in English, ask your partner or look in your dictionary. Then write your new words on page 191.

   1. What is the man wearing?

   2. What is the man doing?

   3. What is the dolphin doing?

B. Work in pairs or small groups. Ask and answer the questions.

   1. Do you have a pet? If so, what kind? If not, would you like to have a pet?

   2. Do you think a human and an animal can have a true friendship? Explain your answer.

The Best-Dressed Penguin

> PREPARE TO READ

A. Look at the words (and phrases) in the list. Write the number(s) next to each word to show what you know. You may be able to write more than one number next to some of the words. You will study all of these words in this chapter.

1. I can use the word in a sentence.

2. I know <u>one meaning</u> of the word.

3. I know <u>more than one meaning</u> of the word.

4. I know how to pronounce the word.

B. Work with a partner. Look at the picture. Ask and answer the questions. If you don't know a word in English, ask your partner or look in your dictionary. Then write your new words on page 191.

1. What is the penguin wearing?

2. Why do you think he's wearing it?

3. What is the woman's job?

_____ accept

_____ each other

_____ famous

_____ fashionable

_____ feel sorry for

_____ identify

_____ leader

_____ recognize

_____ stranger

_____ treat

Reading Skill: Understanding Pronouns

Pronouns refer to nouns. When writers do not want to repeat a noun, they use a pronoun to replace it. When you see a pronoun, ask yourself, "Which noun does this pronoun refer to or replace?"

EXAMPLE:

noun   pronoun

Pam Schaller is a scientist. She works at the California Academy of Sciences.

Subject pronouns	Object pronouns	Other pronouns
I	me	each other
you	you	one
he/she/it	him/her/it	ones
we	us	
they	them	

C. Read the first paragraph of the newspaper article "The Best-Dressed Penguin" on the next page. Then answer the questions.

   1. Who is Pierre?

   2. Which pronoun does the writer use to refer to Pierre?

   3. What does the pronoun *it* refer to?

 **READ**

Read "The Best-Dressed Penguin." As you read, circle the pronouns.

The Best-Dressed Penguin

1 Pierre is a penguin. He lives at an animal research[1] center in San Francisco, California. In 2007, Pierre became **famous** for being the best-dressed[2] penguin in the world. (Well, in fact, he
5 was the world's *only* dressed penguin …) Pierre's outfit?[3] No, it wasn't a tuxedo. It was a wet suit.

Pam Schaller is a scientist at the California Academy of Sciences, where Pierre lives. She explains that penguins lose all of their feathers[4]
10 and grow new ones every year. In 2005, Pierre did not get any new feathers. By 2007, he was bald[5] on many parts of his body.

This was a serious problem for Pierre. Before he lost his feathers, he was a group
15 **leader**. But when he went bald, the other penguins started to **treat** him badly. That is because they could not **identify** him. Penguins identify **each other** by their feathers. The other penguins were treating Pierre like a **stranger**
20 because they did not **recognize** him.

Another problem for Pierre was the cold. Penguins love to swim, but they need their feathers to stay warm. Pierre was too cold to swim very much. Pierre's situation was
25 dangerous. It did not look like he could survive.

Luckily for Pierre, he had a clever friend: Pam Schaller. Pam **felt sorry for** Pierre, and she wanted to help him. Then she got an idea. Maybe she could make Pierre a wet suit. That
30 way, he could enjoy swimming again. She got the idea from looking at her own wet suit and clothes for dogs.

Pierre wore his wet suit for about six weeks. He started swimming again, and the
35 other penguins seemed to like his new outfit. They **accepted** him back into the group. And then something even better happened. Pierre's feathers grew back! Pam removed his wet suit, and he became a group leader again.

40 What's next for the world's only dressed penguin? Maybe it's time for something less practical and more **fashionable**. Hmm … maybe a tuxedo?

---

[1] **research:** serious study of a subject
[2] **best-dressed:** wearing very nice clothes
[3] **outfit:** clothes worn together
[4] **feathers:** light soft things that cover a bird's body
[5] **bald:** having little or no hair on your head or body

Vocabulary Check

Complete the sentences with the boldfaced words from the reading.

1. Look at you! You're a big girl now! I didn't _____ you at first!

2. I like your new shoes. They are very _____. Where did you buy them?

3. Why were you talking to that _____? I told you not to talk to people you don't know!

4. They got married because they love _____.

5. I'm the _____. Follow me!

6. He doesn't _____ his friends very well. He makes fun of them all the time.

7. He is a(n) _____ actor. All over the world, people recognize him.

8. The police officers asked the five men a lot of questions. They were trying to _____ the man who took my money.

9. It is hard to get into that school. Last year, they _____ only 25 percent of the students who wanted to go there.

10. The other children were making fun of her. I helped her because I _____ her.

> READ AGAIN

Read "The Best-Dressed Penguin" again and complete the comprehension exercises on the next page. As you work, keep the reading goal in mind.

READING GOAL: To explain the story behind the picture on page 60

Comprehension Check

A. Find the sentences in the reading. What do the underlined pronouns refer to? Circle the letter of the correct answer. The numbers in parentheses are the paragraphs where you can find the sentences.

1. She explains that penguins lose all of their feathers and grow new <u>ones</u> every year. (2)
   Ones refers to _____.

   a. penguins   **b.** all   **c.** feathers

2. Penguins identify <u>each other</u> by their feathers. (3)
   Each other refers to _____.

   a. feathers   **b.** other penguins   **c.** strangers

3. The other penguins were treating Pierre like a stranger because they did not recognize <u>him</u>. (3)
   Him refers to _____.

   a. a stranger   **b.** Pierre   **c.** another penguin

B. Look at the picture on page 60. Read the sentences. Decide whether the sentence happened before the picture, at the time of the picture, or after the picture. Write *B* (before), *T* (at the time), or *A* (after). There may be more than one answer.

_____*B, T*_____ **1.** Pierre is bald.

_____ **2.** Pam Schaller feels sorry for Pierre.

_____ **3.** Pam Schaller makes a wet suit for Pierre.

_____ **4.** Other penguins treat Pierre like a stranger.

_____ **5.** Pierre's feathers grow back.

_____ **6.** The group accepts Pierre.

_____ **7.** Pierre enjoys swimming.

_____ **8.** Pierre doesn't need a wet suit.

C. Imagine that a friend asks you to explain the picture of Pierre in his wet suit. Write the story on the lines. Use the words in the list. Do not look back at the reading.

accept	identify	recognize	treat
each other	leader	scientist	wet suit
feathers	penguin	stranger	

_____

_____

_____

_____

_____

_____

_____

_____

_____

_____

_____

_____

_____

_____

> ## DISCUSS

Work in small groups. Ask and answer the questions.

1. What is your favorite animal? Why is it your favorite?

2. Do you dislike any animals? Which one(s)? Why?

3. Do you know any unusual true stories about animals? Tell the group.

Christian the Lion

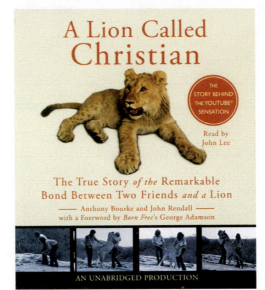

> PREPARE TO READ

A. Look at the words (and phrases) in the list. Write the number(s) next to each word to show what you know. You may be able to write more than one number next to some of the words. You will study all of these words in this chapter.

1. I can use the word in a sentence.

2. I know <u>one meaning</u> of the word.

3. I know <u>more than one meaning</u> of the word.

4. I know how to pronounce the word.

B. Work in small groups. Talk about the picture. Think of a story that could explain what is happening. If you don't know a word in English, ask your classmate or look in your dictionary. Then write your new words on page 191.

C. Preview the story "Christian the Lion" on the next page. Where do you think this story came from? Circle the letter of your answer.

a. a book on animal and human friendship

b. the fashion section of a newspaper

c. a travel guide to London

d. the Web page of the animal behavior department at a university

_____ alone

_____ appear

_____ convince

_____ department store

_____ hear about

_____ hug

_____ owner

_____ ride

_____ throw

_____ toward

READ

Read "Christian the Lion." Was the story you imagined for Exercise B similar to the real story?

෨ Christian the Lion ⊗

1   In 1969, King's Road was a very fashionable street in London. Many famous people lived there. For a year, a lion named Christian did, too. He **rode** around in a Mercedes Benz. He went to expensive restaurants. His picture **appeared** in a fashion advertisement.[1]

5   Christian's **owners**, Ace Bourke and John Rendall, bought him at Harrods **department store**. The little lion was all **alone** in the exotic[2] animal department, and they felt sorry for him. Of course, today you cannot buy a wild animal in a department store. But London was a pretty wild place in the 1960s!

    Bourke and Rendall were working in a shop on King's Road at the time. They

10 **convinced** the shop's owner that the little cub would be good for business. Christian moved into the shop's basement.[3] On Sundays, Christian slept in the shop window. For exercise, Rendall and Bourke played soccer with Christian and took him swimming in the English Channel.[4] They loved the little cub, but Christian was growing fast. He could not stay with them forever.

15   Then Bourke and Rendall **heard about** a wildlife conservationist[5] in Kenya. His name was George Adamson, and he knew a lot about lions. Bourke and Rendall asked for his help. Adamson agreed to try to introduce Christian to the wild, and Bourke and Rendall took Christian to Kenya. It was hard to say goodbye, but they knew it was the best thing for Christian.

20   In 1972, the two men went back for a visit. Adamson did not think that Christian would recognize them, but he was wrong. Rendall and Bourke filmed[6] the emotional moment when Christian saw them. Rendall says, "We called him and he … started to walk **toward** us very slowly. Then … he ran toward us, … **hugged** us … **threw** himself onto us with his paws on our shoulders. Everyone

25 was crying."*

    Rendall saw Christian for the last time in 1974. Christian was a wild lion by then, with his own family. But he still remembered his old friend. After that last visit, no one ever saw Christian again, but Bourke and Rendall are convinced that he lived a long, happy life in the wild.

30   (*You can watch a video of that emotional moment at www.youtube.com. Type the words "Christian the Lion" in the search bar.)

---

[1] **advertisement:** a picture with words intended to persuade people to buy something

[2] **exotic:** unusual and exciting

[3] **basement:** a room in a building that is below the level of the ground

[4] **English Channel:** the part of the Atlantic Ocean that separates England from northern France

[5] **conservationist:** a person who protects natural things such as animals, plants, and forests

[6] **film:** use a camera to make a movie

Vocabulary Check

Circle the letter of the correct answer to complete each sentence. The boldfaced words are the target words.

1. I went to a **department store** because I needed to buy _____.

   a. some medicine   **b.** shoes and a   **c.** something for dinner
   watch

2. If your name **appears** on a list, it _____ there.

   a. is written   **b.** was always   **c.** is the only name

3. When you **throw** a ball, you use your arm. When you **throw** yourself onto someone, you use your _____.

   a. fingers   **b.** body   **c.** brain

4. He **convinced** me to go. I _____.

   a. didn't go   **b.** didn't want to   **c.** always wanted to go
   go at first

5. He lives **alone**. He doesn't _____ his apartment.

   a. share   **b.** rent   **c.** like

6. People do not usually **hug** if they _____.

   a. are strangers   **b.** know each other   **c.** love each other

7. I just **heard about** her new job. I _____ a few minutes ago.

   a. found her   **b.** found out   **c.** listened to her
   about it

8. He **rode** in the _____, and I drove.

   a. driver's seat   **b.** back seat   **c.** street

9. He _____ her, so he ran **toward** her.

   a. wanted to feel   **b.** wanted to get   **c.** wanted to hug
   sorry for   away from

10. He isn't the **owner** of the car, so he can't _____.

    a. buy it   **b.** sell it   **c.** ride in it

► READ AGAIN

Read "Christian the Lion" again and complete the comprehension exercises. As you work, keep the reading goal in mind.

> 📖 **READING GOAL:** To tell Christian's life story

Comprehension Check

A. Find the sentences in the reading. What do the underlined words refer to? Circle the letter of the correct answer. The numbers in parentheses are the paragraphs where you can find the sentences.

1. Christian's owners, Ace Bourke and John Rendall, bought <u>him</u> at Harrods department store. (2)
   Him refers to _____.
   a. Christian's owner   **b.** John Rendall   **c.** Christian

2. It was hard to say good-bye, but <u>they</u> knew it was the best thing for Christian. (4)
   They refers to _____.
   a. Adamson and Bourke   **b.** Rendall and Christian   **c.** Bourke and Rendall

3. Adamson did not think that Christian would recognize <u>them</u>, but <u>he</u> was wrong. (5)
   Them refers to _____.
   a. Bourke and Rendall   **b.** Adamson, Bourke, and Rendall   **c.** Bourke

   He refers to _____.
   d. Christian   **e.** Adamson   **f.** Rendall

4. But <u>he</u> still remembered <u>his old friend</u>. (6)
   He refers to _____ .
   a. Bourke   **b.** Rendall   **c.** Christian

   His old friend refers to _____ .
   d. Bourke   **e.** Rendall   **f.** Christian

B. Put the events from the story in the correct order. Write *1* for the first thing that happened, *2* for the second thing, and so on.

___1___ Two men bought a lion cub at a department store in London.

_____ The men visited Christian, and the lion was happy to see them.

_____ The men heard about George Adamson.

_____ Christian became a wild lion and had his own family.

_____ Rendall visited Christian again, and Christian recognized him.

_____ The men left Christian in Kenya.

_____ The men asked Adamson for his help with Christian.

_____ The cub became too big to live with the men.

_____ The men took Christian to Africa.

_____ The lion lived in a shop in London.

C. Close your books. Sit in a circle in small groups. Tell Christian's life story. One student will start and say one or two sentences. The next student will continue the story, and so on. If someone makes a mistake, correct it before continuing the story.

> DISCUSS

Read the statements. Do you agree or disagree? Write a number for your opinion. Then talk in small groups. Explain your opinions.

strongly agree   unsure   strongly disagree

⟵ 1   2   3   4   5 ⟶

_____ **a.** Wild animals and humans can never be friends.

_____ **b.** It is wrong to buy and sell wild animals.

_____ **c.** It is wrong to put wild animals in the zoo.

_____ **d.** The "love" between a human and an animal is not real love.

_____ **e.** I could love an animal in the same way that I love a friend.

> VOCABULARY SKILL BUILDING

> ## Vocabulary Skill: The Prefix *dis-*
>
> A *prefix* is a word part that is added to the beginning of some words. Prefixes don't change the form of the word. They change the meaning. For example, the prefix *dis-* means *not*. Sometimes *dis-* gives a word the opposite meaning. Other times the new meaning is different, but not opposite.
>
> **EXAMPLE:**
>
> opposite meaning: *like*/**dis***like* = not like
>
> different meaning, but not opposite: *appear*/**dis***appear* = go out of sight suddenly

A. Create new words with the prefix *dis-* and the boldfaced words. Use these new words to complete the sentences. The boldfaced words are target words from this chapter and previous chapters.

1. I don't **agree** with you. We _____ with each other.

2. The boy **infected** his sister with his cold. The mother _____ the cut on her child's knee.

3. Your idea is not **similar** to mine. Our ideas are _____.

4. When you are looking for a job, a college degree is an **advantage**. If you don't have a college degree, it is a _____.

5. He **covered** up the truth. The police never _____ that he lied.

6. He **owned** a lot of land, but he didn't leave it to his daughter. He _____ her and left all of his land to his son.

B. Read the sentences in Exercise A again. Then circle the letter of the correct meaning for each word.

1. disagree
   a. not agree
   b. change your opinion

2. disinfect
   a. not infect
   b. clean

3. dissimilar
   a. not similar
   b. changed

4. disadvantage
   a. not an advantage
   b. a change from good to bad

5. discover
   a. not cover
   b. find out

6. disown
   a. not own
   b. end a relationship with your child

Learn the Vocabulary

Using a Dictionary: Verb Forms

Verbs are listed in an English-English dictionary in their *base form*. The base form is the simplest form of the verb, with no ending.

Irregular verbs
In most dictionaries, the simple past and past participle forms of irregular verbs are listed next to the base form of the verb.

> **ride¹** /raɪd/ *v.* (past tense **rode** /roʊd/, past participle **ridden** /ˈrɪdn/) **1** [I,T] to sit on an animal, especially a horse, or on a bicycle, and make it move along: *He rode his bike to school.* | *In the movies, the bad guys* **ride on** *black horses.* **2** [I,T] to travel in a car, train, or other vehicle → DRIVE: *We rode the bus into New York City.* | *Mrs. Turnbull rode in silence.* | *My three-year-old loves to ride the escalators in Bloomingdale's.* **3 let sth ride** (spoken) to take no action about something that is wrong or unpleasant: *I didn't like what he was saying, but I let it ride.* **4** [T] (spoken) to annoy someone by continuously criticizing him/her or asking him/her to do a lot of things: *Why are you riding her so hard?* [ORIGIN: Old English *ridan*]

If the verb is irregular and you don't know the base form, look up the past tense form. There you will see the base form of the verb.

> **rode** /roʊd/ *v.* the past tense of RIDE

Regular verbs
For regular verbs that change spelling when you add *-ed*, the spelling of the past forms is listed next to the base form of the verb.

> **hug¹** /hʌg/ *v.* (**hugged, hugging**) [T] **1** to put your arms around someone and hold him/her tightly to show love or friendship: *Hug your children.*
>
> **THESAURUS**
>
> **embrace** – to put your arms around someone and hold him/her in a caring way: *Jason warmly embraced his son.*
> **cuddle** – to put your arms around someone or something as a sign of love: *Dawn and her boyfriend were cuddling on the sofa.*
> **hold** – to have something firmly in your hands or arms: *She held the baby in her arms.*
> **wrap your arms around sb** – to hold someone in a loving way by putting your arms around his or her body: *I wrapped my arms around my daughter as she cried.*

For regular verbs with NO changes in spelling, the past forms are NOT listed.

A. Look up the verbs in your dictionary. Complete the chart.

Base form	Simple past	Past participle
accept		
appear	*appeared*	*appeared*
control	*controlled*	
convince		
	felt	
hug		
identify		
lead		
recognize		
ride	rode	
	threw	
treat		

B. Complete the chart with the verbs from Exercise A. Write the base form of the verbs.

Regular verb, no spelling changes	Regular verb, spelling changes	Irregular verbs
accept	*control*	*ride*

C. Make cards for the words that were new to you in Chapters 9 and 10. Include target words and words that you wrote on page 191. If the new word is a verb, write both the base form and the past tense form on the card.

D. Go back to the vocabulary list at the beginning of each chapter. What did you learn about the target words? Add your numbers to the lists.

Vocabulary Practice 5, see page 197

UNIT 6 | Learning from Mother Nature

> THINK BEFORE YOU READ

A. Work with a partner. Look at the picture. Ask and answer the questions. If you don't know a word in English, ask your partner or look in your dictionary. Then write your new words on page 191.

1. Where are the people in the picture? What are they doing?

2. The title of the unit is "Learning from Mother Nature." What do you think the title means?

B. Check (✓) the statements you agree with. Then share your answers in small groups.

_____ **1.** When I have free time, I like to spend it outside, in nature.

_____ **2.** I like to read and watch programs about nature.

_____ **3.** I know a lot about nature.

11 Natural by Design

PREPARE TO READ

A. Look at the words in the list. Write the number(s) next to each word to show what you know. You may be able to write more than one number next to some of the words. You will study all of these words in this chapter.

1. I can use the word in a sentence.

2. I know <u>one meaning</u> of the word.

3. I know <u>more than one meaning</u> of the word.

4. I know how to pronounce the word.

B. Work with a partner. Look at the pictures. Ask and answer the questions. If you don't know a word in English, ask your partner or look in your dictionary. Then write your new words on page 191.

1. In what ways are the fish and the car similar?

2. What do you think a car designer could learn from studying a fish? Check (✓) your answer(s).

How to make the car . . .

_____ **a.** more powerful   _____ **d.** safer

_____ **b.** look better   _____ **e.** go faster

_____ **c.** use less energy

_____ building

_____ copy

_____ design

_____ efficient

_____ evolution

_____ heat

_____ pressure

_____ protect

_____ rise

_____ temperature

Reading Skill: Understanding Examples

Examples help readers understand difficult ideas. A reading often starts with a short explanation of an idea, followed by an example. Don't worry if you do not understand the explanation at first. When you finish reading the examples, go back and read the explanation again. It should be easier to understand.

C. Preview the Web page "Natural by Design." Then answer the questions.

1. What is the main topic of the Web page? (It is OK if you don't understand what it means yet.)

2. How many examples are there to explain the main topic?

> READ

Read "Natural by Design." Were your answers for Exercise C correct?

http://www.biomimicryfacts.com

NATURAL BY DESIGN

1 **BIOMIMICRY: The Way of the Future!**
BIOMIMICRY FAQs

What is biomimicry?
Bio- means *life*, and *mimic* means *copy*.
5 Biomimicry is the science of **copying** living things in the natural world. Through thousands of years of **evolution**, nature has found the simplest, most **efficient** ways to do many things. And it does most of them
10 in a way that is safe for the environment.[1] **Designers** who use biomimicry study nature. They find answers to today's problems in the natural world.

Can you give some examples of
15 ***biomimicry?***
There are many examples. Here are two.

Ex. 1: Car/Boxfish
In 2005, DaimlerChrysler designed a new car. It has many of the same characteristics as
20 the boxfish. Both the boxfish and the car are energy-efficient, powerful, and fast. They can move well in small places. They are able to survive a lot of **pressure** (from water or wind), and they have a strong outside covering. The
25 covering **protects** what is inside of them.

Ex. 2: Building/Termite[2] Mound[3]
When an architect[4] in Zimbabwe, Africa, was designing an office **building**, he got ideas from an African termite mound. This
30 kind of African termite survives by eating the mold[5] that grows inside its mound. The mold only grows if the **temperature** inside the

---

[1] **environment:** the land, water, and air in which people, animals, and plants live

[2] **termite:** an insect that eats wood from trees or buildings

[3] **mound:** a pile of dirt, sand, etc.

[4] **architect:** someone who designs buildings

[5] **mold:** a soft green or black substance that grows on old food and on objects in warm, wet places

mound never changes. But it is very hot in Zimbabwe. Why doesn't the mound get hotter
35 and hotter during the day? The termites control the temperature.

How do they do it? Termites build their mounds so that air enters under the ground. Why? It is colder underground
40 than on the land's surface. As the cool air **rises**, it cools the inside of the mound. If the air temperature inside the mound gets too cool, the termites make holes[6] in the walls. Then hot air from the outside enters
45 the mound. If the air inside gets too hot, the termites close the holes.

To make the office building energy efficient, the architect designed it like a termite mound. Air enters the building

50 under the ground. Then vents (holes) in the building open and close all day to control the temperature. The building costs 90 percent less to **heat** and cool than similar buildings in the same city.

[6] **hole:** an empty or open space in something solid

Vocabulary Check

Circle the letter of the correct answer to complete each sentence. The boldfaced words are the target words.

1. You need to **heat** water to make _____.
   a. juice   **b.** soda   **c.** tea

2. The teacher will _____ you if you **copy** a classmate's homework.
   a. apologize to   **b.** feel sorry for   **c.** punish

3. The _____ **rises** in the morning.
   a. air   **b.** moon   **c.** sun

4. When the **temperature** goes down, we feel _____.
   a. cooler   **b.** hotter   **c.** warmer

5. _____ are **buildings**.
   a. Elevators   **b.** Houses   **c.** Swimming pools

(continued on next page)

6. Mothers **protect** their children from _____.

    a. danger   **b.** safety   **c.** survival

7. Fashion **designers** _____ pictures of clothes.

    a. buy   **b.** own   **c.** draw

8. Changes in air **pressure** in an airplane can make your ears _____.

    a. grow   **b.** hear better   **c.** hurt

9. Through **evolution**, plants and animals _____.

    a. change   **b.** exercise   **c.** get bigger

10. She's **efficient**. She completes her work _____.

    a. quickly   **b.** naturally   **c.** safely

> READ AGAIN

Read "Natural by Design" again and complete the comprehension exercises. As you work, keep the reading goal in mind.

> **READING GOAL:** To identify some examples of biomimicry

Comprehension Check

A. Complete the chart on the next page with the words and phrases from the list.

air enters underground	fast
air vents open and close	inside temperature doesn't change
biomimicry	moves well in small spaces
~~boxfish~~	office building
can take a lot of pressure	powerful
car	protective covering
~~energy efficient~~	termite mound

Examples of _____		
Human-made	**Natural**	**Characteristics (copied by designers)**
_____	*boxfish*	*energy-efficient*
_____	_____	_____

B. Check (✓) the examples of biomimicry.

_____ **1.** Designers of a new car give it the name of the world's fastest land animal, the cheetah.

_____ **2.** A bird finds a newspaper on the ground. It uses it to build a nest.

(continued on next page)

3. Architects design a building in a city with a lot of earthquakes. The building has pieces of steel underground, like the roots of a tree.

4. Scientists study spiderwebs. Then they make a new material that is very light and very strong, like spiderwebs.

C. Work with a partner. Compare your answers for Exercise B.

> DISCUSS

Work in small groups. Think of two human-made objects (things) that were designed through biomimicry. What are the products? Which plant or animal did the designer copy? What characteristics are similar? Complete the chart.

Product	Plant or animal	Characteristics

Swarm Intelligence

> PREPARE TO READ

A. Look at the words in the list. Write the number(s) next to each word to show what you know. You may be able to write more than one number next to some of the words. You will study all of these words in this chapter.

1. I can use the word in a sentence.

2. I know <u>one meaning</u> of the word.

3. I know <u>more than one meaning</u> of the word.

4. I know how to pronounce the word.

_____ chance

_____ collect

_____ fight

_____ illness

_____ intelligence

_____ organized

_____ path

_____ rule

_____ solve

_____ without

B. Work with a partner. Look at the pictures. Then do the activities below. If you don't know a word in English, ask your partner or look in your dictionary. Then write your new words on page 191.

1. Label the picture. Write the words in English for what you see.

2. Put the pictures in order. Write *1* for the first picture, *2* for the second, and so on. Don't look at the reading. You will have a chance to check the order after you read.

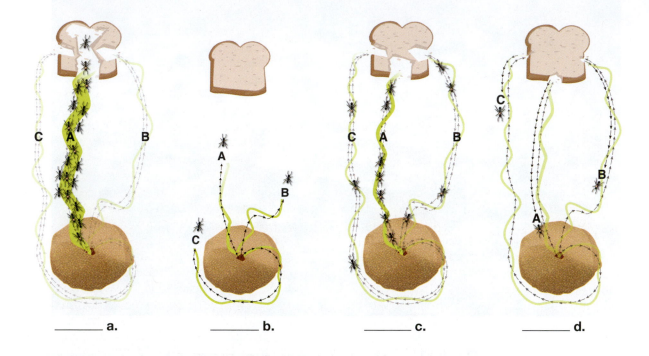

_____ a.   _____ b.   _____ c.   _____ d.

Reading Skill: Visualizing

When you read, it is helpful to make a picture in your head of what the writer is explaining or describing. This is called *visualizing*. If your "picture" doesn't make sense, then you probably didn't understand something in the reading. Go back and read again, and correct the picture in your head.

C. Preview the newspaper article "Swarm Intelligence" on the next page. Which paragraph do the pictures above go with? Check (✓) that paragraph in the reading.

READ

Read "Swarm Intelligence." As you read the paragraph that goes with the pictures, check the order of your pictures in Exercise B on page 82. If you made a mistake, correct it.

Swarm Intelligence

1　　The next time you see an ant in your kitchen, think twice before you kill it. Why? Scientists believe that ants may one day help us **solve** some serious problems.

5　　Ants live in large groups. They have very small brains and no leader. But as a group, they are **organized**, efficient, and excellent at solving problems. For example, they are always able to find the fastest way to get to
10　food, and thousands of them can travel to the same place **without** getting into a traffic jam.[1] How can they do this with such small brains?

　　The answer is simple. Any one ant doesn't
15　need to know much; it just needs a few simple **rules**. When it follows those rules, it becomes one small part of a large group brain. This is called *swarm intelligence*.

　　We're going to look at an example of
20　swarm intelligence, but first, here are the rules:

　　1. When an ant finds food, it doesn't eat it. It takes it back to the nest.[2]
　　2. Ants give off[3] a special smell when
25　　　they find food.
　　3. Ants always follow that special smell.

　　Now, let's see what happens when a swarm of ants follows these three simple rules.

　　Several ants find some bread. They each
30　take a little of the bread back to the nest. By **chance**, one of the ants takes the shortest, fastest **path** and gets to the nest first. The other ants at the nest don't know that's the best path to the food, but they don't need
35　to. They just need to follow the rules. They follow the smell of that ant back to the bread. When they find the bread, they add their smell to the path. This path, the shortest, fastest path to a meal, now has the strongest
40　smell. It becomes the main path for all of the ants. Simple, efficient—and very intelligent.

　　Today, scientists are making simple robots that work in swarms, like ants. One day, they hope to use these robots to **collect**
45　information in dangerous places. They also think that the cells[4] in our bodies might use swarm intelligence. If so, the lessons we have learned from ants might one day help us **fight** cancer[5] and other serious **illnesses**.

---

[1] **traffic jam:** a long line of vehicles on the road that cannot move, or that moves very slowly

[2] **nest:** a place where insects or small ants live

[3] **give off:** produce

[4] **cell:** the smallest part of any living thing

[5] **cancer:** a disease in which cells in one part of the body grow in a way that is not normal

Vocabulary Check

Circle the letter of the correct answer to complete each sentence. The boldfaced words are the target words.

1. When you have a serious **illness**, you are _____.
   - **a.** a survivor
   - **b.** alone
   - **c.** very sick

2. If you go **without** food, you eat _____.
   - **a.** a lot
   - **b.** nothing
   - **c.** something

3. A person of high **intelligence** is considered to be _____.
   - **a.** clean
   - **b.** serious
   - **c.** smart

4. There is a **path**. You can _____ on it.
   - **a.** live
   - **b.** walk
   - **c.** swim

5. Please **collect** your things before you leave the plane. Don't _____ anything.
   - **a.** copy
   - **b.** leave
   - **c.** remove

6. Before you can play a game, you need to _____ the **rules**.
   - **a.** change
   - **b.** prepare
   - **c.** understand

7. She is a very _____ person. Her desk is always **organized**.
   - **a.** famous
   - **b.** humorous
   - **c.** neat

8. Without intelligence, it is _____ to **solve** a problem.
   - **a.** difficult
   - **b.** efficient
   - **c.** fun

9. Sleep and medicine helped me to **fight** my cold. Now I feel _____.
   - **a.** healthy
   - **b.** tired
   - **c.** ill

10. We won by **chance**. We were _____.
    - **a.** lucky
    - **b.** serious
    - **c.** the best players

> READ AGAIN

Read "Swarm Intelligence" again and complete the comprehension exercises on the next page. As you work, keep the reading goal in mind.

> 📖 **READING GOAL:** To understand what swarm intelligence is and identify examples of it

Comprehension Check

A. Read the statements about ants. Write *T* (true) or *F* (false).

_____ **1.** They live in large groups.

_____ **2.** They think before they act.

_____ **3.** They follow rules.

_____ **4.** They share information with each other.

_____ **5.** They follow one leader.

_____ **6.** They have no leader.

_____ **7.** They are very efficient at collecting food.

_____ **8.** They take a long time to find the best path to food.

B. Circle the letter of the correct answer to complete each sentence about swarm intelligence. There is only one correct answer.

1. The activity is always _____ for the group's survival.

   a. difficult   **b.** good   **c.** fun

2. The rules are _____.

   a. difficult   **b.** easy   **c.** strange

3. The members of the group _____ follow the rules.

   a. always   **b.** sometimes   **c.** never

4. There is _____ of the activity.

   a. a group of leaders   **b.** one leader   **c.** no leader

5. The group members do not _____ what they are doing.

   a. like   **b.** remember   **c.** think about

6. The group is more intelligent than the _____.

   a. leaders   **b.** members   **c.** other groups

C. Check (✓) the groups that are using swarm intelligence. Use the statements from Exercise B to help you decide. When you finish, discuss your answers with a partner.

_____ **1.** Wolves get together to hunt.

_____ **2.** A group of cattle jumps off a cliff.

(continued on next page)

_____ **3.** A group of fish changes direction to get away from a hungry dolphin.

_____ **4.** Hundreds of birds all sit on the roof of the same building.

_____ **5.** Different robots do different jobs at an automobile factory.

_____ **6.** A group of bees moves to a new hive in a better location.

> DISCUSS

Work in small groups. Ask and answer the questions.

1. Reread the last paragraph of "Swarm Intelligence." What kind of information do you think a group of robots could collect, and where?

2. Do large groups of people ever behave like a swarm? If you answer yes, give an example.

3. What other animals and insects have swarm intelligence? Write two more examples.

a. _____   **b.** _____

> VOCABULARY SKILL BUILDING

Vocabulary Skill: Collocations

Words often go together, or *collocate*, with other words. This means that one word is often used with another word. When you learn a new word, it is helpful to learn its collocations—that is, the other words that are often used with that word. Learning common collocations will help you use words the way native English speakers do. For example, English speakers say *tall building*, not *high building*. Some common collocation patterns appear in the following chart:

Parts of speech	Example
preposition + noun	by chance
verb + noun	follow a rule
noun + noun	traffic jam
adjective + noun	serious illness

A. Scan "Swarm Intelligence" for the words below. Write the collocations.

1. _____*by*_____ chance

2. _____*follow*_____ a rule

3. _____ an illness

4. solve _____

5. collect _____

6. _____ intelligence

7. _____ a lesson

8. get into a _____

B. Write your own sentences with the collocations from Exercise A.

1. _____

2. _____

3. _____

4. _____

5. _____

6. _____

7. _____

8. _____

Learn the Vocabulary

Using a Dictionary: Collocations

You can find common collocations in the dictionary. They usually appear boldfaced in the example sentences.

> **rule**[1] /rul/ *n.* **1** [C] an official instruction that says how something is to be done or what is allowed, especially in a game, organization, or job: *Erin knows the **rules of** the game.* | ***strict rules** about what you can wear* | *If you **follow** the **rules**, you won't get into trouble.* | *Well, that's what happens if you **break** the **rules** (=disobey them).* | *It's **against the rules** to pick up the ball (=it is not allowed).* |

> **tem·pera·ture** /'tɛmprətʃɚ/ *n.* **1** [C,U] how hot or cold something is: *Water freezes **at a temperature of** 32°F.* | *The **temperature rose** to 102 degrees.* | ***Temperatures** could **drop** to below zero tonight.* | *Store this product at **room temperature** (=the normal temperature in a room).* **2 sb's temperature** the temperature of your body, used as a measure of whether you are sick or not: *The nurse **took** my **temperature**.* **3 have a temperature** to be hot because you are sick

A. Read the dictionary entries for *rule* and *temperature*. Complete the sentences with the correct collocations.

1. If you _____ the rules, I will punish you.

2. It is _____ the rules to drive without a license.

3. They are very responsible. They always _____ the rules.

4. It got really hot. The temperature _____ to 104° F (40° C).

5. It's getting cold. The temperature will _____ to 32° F (0° C).

6. I'm ill. I _____ a temperature. I'm going to stay home today.

7. She felt sick, so the doctor _____ her temperature.

8. The fruit tastes better cold than at _____ temperature.

B. Go back to the list at the beginning of each chapter. What did you learn about the target words? Add your numbers to the lists.

Vocabulary Practice 6, see page 198

FLUENCY PRACTICE 2

Fluency Strategy

To read more fluently, you should not read word by word. You should read in phrases (groups of words). Try these strategies to stop yourself from reading word by word:

- Do not point your finger or your pencil at each word as you read it. If you need to use your finger or pencil to keep your place, point at the line you are reading and move it down when you finish the line.
- Read with your eyes, not with your mouth. That is, read silently. Do not say the words out loud. If you read out loud, you will be reading every word, rather than whole phrases. It will also slow you down.

It might feel strange or difficult to read this way at first, but as you practice, you will get better at it. You will be reading more quickly and at the same time understanding more. That is, you will be on your way to becoming a fluent reader in English.

> READING 1

Before You Read

A. Read the definition of *Easter*. You will see this word in the reading.

> Easter: a Christian religious holiday in early spring. At Easter in some countries, parents give their children baskets filled with candy, chocolate rabbits, and colored eggs. Some parents give their children live rabbits or baby chickens or ducks for Easter.

B. Preview "Pinky the Duck, Part 1" on the next page. What kind of story do you think it is? Circle the letter of the correct answer.

   a. a fable about a duck who thought she was human

   b. a true story about a duck and her human family

   c. a newspaper article about a very intelligent duck

Read

A. Read "Pinky the Duck, Part 1." Time yourself. Write your start and end
times and your total reading time. Then calculate your reading speed
(words per minute) and write it in the progress chart on page 205.

Start time: _____ **End time:** _____ **Total time:** _____ (in seconds)

Reading speed:
464 words ÷ _____ (total time in seconds) x 60 = _____ words per minute

✆ Pinky the Duck, Part 1 ✆

1   Sara Savick remembers one special Easter when she was nine years old. Her
parents gave her a baby duckling in a yellow basket.

"Mom said later that she bought the little duck because she felt sorry for it,"
said Sara. The people at the pet store colored the little duckling's feathers pink for
5 Easter. Sara named the duck *Pinky*.

Sara's mother really didn't think that the duckling would survive very long. But
to her surprise, Pinky grew and got stronger and stronger. Soon, the little duckling
was a healthy, hungry duck with white feathers.

"We fed Pinky oatmeal—cooked and uncooked—and small pieces of
10 vegetables," said Sara. Pinky lived inside the house with Sara and her family. The
duck went everywhere. She went upstairs and downstairs. She especially loved to
take baths with Sara. Everyone treated Pinky like one of the family.

But just when everything appeared to be perfect, the night of the "talk" came.
Sara's Mom and Dad sat her down. They explained that the best thing for Pinky
15 was to live a normal duck life, with other ducks. It was not natural for ducks to
live indoors with a family, her father told her. He said Pinky needed to swim in
ponds and do all the same things that ducks in the wild do.

Sara started to cry. She was only nine years old, but she understood what was
going to happen. Sara's parents decided to take Pinky to a park that was about two
20 miles away from their home. There was a pond with a lot of other ducks there.
Pinky would have the chance to live a natural life, and Sara could still visit her.

Sara was sad, but she was happy about one thing. At least her parents weren't
going to cook and eat Pinky!

The next day was Sunday, the big day. Sara and her parents put Pinky in a box
25 and drove to the park. Sara said that Pinky did not look very happy. In Sara's
opinion, Pinky was convinced that she was a human, not a duck. Later Sara learned
that ducks will follow the first animal, person, or thing that they see, convinced
that it is their mother. And when Pinky was only a day or so old, she went to live
with Sara's family. Naturally, Sara thought, Pinky believed they were her family.

30 Everyone was emotional when they left Pinky at the pond, even Sara's father.
But he tried to convince Sara that Pinky was fine. As Sara walked toward the car,
she looked over her shoulder. She saw Pinky standing alone. The other ducks were
swimming around in circles, looking at Pinky. To Sara, it looked like they were
trying to identify the strange animal. They didn't recognize Pinky as a duck.

B. Read "Pinky the Duck, Part 1" again, a little faster this time. Write your start and end times and your total reading time. Then calculate your reading speed (words per minute) and write it in the progress chart on page 205.

Start time: _____   **End time:** _____   **Total time:** _____ (in seconds)

Reading speed:
464 words ÷ _____ (total time in seconds) x 60 = _____ words per minute

Comprehension Check

A. Read the statements about the reading. Write *T* (true) or *F* (false).

_____ **1.** Pinky was born with pink feathers.

_____ **2.** Sara named her duckling Pinky because of the color of her feathers.

_____ **3.** Sara's mother did not think that the little duckling would live very long.

_____ **4.** Pinky ate a lot and grew up to be a healthy duck.

_____ **5.** Pinky lived outside the house in the garden.

_____ **6.** Pinky and Sara sometimes took a bath together.

_____ **7.** Sara's parents didn't want Pinky anymore because she was dirty.

_____ **8.** Sara's parents wanted to cook and eat Pinky, but Sara convinced them not to.

_____ **9.** Sara's parents thought Pinky's life would be better if she lived outside, with wild ducks.

_____ **10.** Ducklings follow the first thing that they see when they are born.

_____ **11.** Ducklings sometimes make a mistake and think people are their mothers.

B. Complete the summary of "Pinky the Duck, Part 1." You will need to write more than one word in some of the spaces.

Sara got a (1) _____ for Easter. She named the duckling

(2) _____. The duckling lived with Sara and her family in

(3) _____. The duckling grew and became a

(4) _____. The duck could go (5) _____ in the

house. She loved to (6) _____ with Sara. Everyone

(7) _____ the duck like one of the family. But when

the duck got older, Sara's (8) _____ decided the duck

needed to live with (9) _____. They took the duck to a

(10) _____ that was about (11) _____ from

their house. They left the duck there with (12) _____. Sara

felt (13) _____, but her parents told her she could

(14) _____ the duck at the park.

C. Check your answers for the comprehension questions in the Answer Key
on page 206. Then calculate your score and write it in the progress chart
on page 205.

_____ (my number correct) ÷ 25 x 100 = _____%

> READING 2

Before You Read

What will happen in "Pinky the Duck, Part 2?" Make two predictions.

1. _____

2. _____

Read

A. Read "Pinky the Duck, Part 2." Time yourself. Write your start and end
times and your total reading time. Then calculate your reading speed
(words per minute) and write it in the progress chart on page 205.

Start time: _____ **End time:** _____ **Total time:** _____ (in seconds)

Reading speed:
371 words ÷ _____ (total time in seconds) x 60 = _____ words per minute

ॐ Pinky the Duck, Part 2 ॐ

1   The next morning, Sara was getting ready for school when she looked out the
kitchen window. She couldn't believe her eyes! There was Pinky, happily walking
around in the grass. The park was two miles away. Sara imagined Pinky walking
alone on the busy city streets to get home. (Pinky couldn't fly because Sara's
5 father had clipped her wings.)
      Sara was sure her parents would agree to keep Pinky. It was clear that Pinky
didn't want to be with the other ducks. What if she tried to walk home again? It
was dangerous for her to be on the city streets. But Sara could not convince her
father. He drove Pinky back to the pond, and told her to stay, as you might say to
10 a dog. Then he got back in the car and took Sara to school. Sara cried so much she
made herself ill.

The next morning, Sara got up and looked out the window. There was Pinky again, outside on the grass! When Sara's father saw her, he waved his arms about wildly, looking at the sky and asking, "How does she do it?"

15   Then he got the box and started to put Pinky in it. But suddenly he threw the box down. Sara saw her chance. She said, "Daddy, Pinky knows her home is with us. She wants to live with us, not some old ducks. She loves us. I love her. I know you and Mommy do, too. Please let her stay. Please—or she'll just get hit by a car some night when she's coming home to us."

20   Then Sara couldn't control her emotions. She got down on the ground next to Pinky and just cried and cried. "Then I saw that Daddy had dropped his arms to his sides, and Mommy was hugging him," Sara remembered.

    Pinky lived with Sara and her family for almost four years. "Pinky had a good life with us," Sara said. "She loved us, and we loved her." Pinky died in
25 her sleep one night. Sara and her parents buried Pinky in the backyard. Sara's mother planted flowers there. Every year at Easter, the flowers come up, and they remember Pinky.

B. Read "Pinky the Duck, Part 2" again, a little faster this time. Write your start and end times and your total reading time. Then calculate your reading speed (words per minute) and write it in the progress chart on page 205.

Start time: _____   **End time:** _____   **Total time:** _____ (in seconds)

Reading speed:
371 words ÷ _____ (total time in seconds) x 60 = _____ words per minute

C. Check the predictions you made on page 92. Were they correct?

Comprehension Check

A. Circle the letter of the correct answer to complete each sentence.

1. Pinky _____ two miles along busy city streets to get back to Sara's house.
   a. flew
   b. ran
   c. walked

2. When she saw Pinky out the kitchen window, Sara _____ to allow Pinky to stay.
   a. asked her mother
   b. convinced her father
   c. tried to convince her father

(continued on next page)

3. Sara's father took Pinky to _____.
   a. the box
   b. Sara's school
   c. the park again

4. The next day, Pinky _____.
   a. came home again
   b. followed Sara to school
   c. got hit by a car

5. Sara's father and mother _____.
   a. decided to allow Sara to keep Pinky
   b. allowed Sara to keep Pinky outside the house
   c. never felt that Pinky was a real part of their family

6. Pinky probably died because she _____.
   a. ate poison
   b. was old
   c. was sleeping

7. In the end, Pinky was really _____.
   a. Easter flowers
   b. a member of the family
   c. a wild duck

B. Check your answers for the comprehension questions in the Answer Key on page 206. Then calculate your score and write it in the progress chart on page 205.

   _____ (my number correct) ÷ 7 x 100 = _____%

Superstitions

> THINK BEFORE YOU READ

A. Work with a partner. Look at the pictures. Ask and answer the questions. If you don't know a word in English, ask your partner or look in your dictionary. Then write your new words on page 192.

    1. What do you see in the pictures? Label the things you know.

    2. Which of these things are bad luck in your culture? Circle them. Which are good luck? Check (✓) them.

B. Complete the chart with information from your culture.

Lucky numbers	Unlucky numbers	Lucky animals	Unlucky animals	Lucky colors	Unlucky colors

C. Work in small groups. Compare the information in your charts. Talk about what is lucky and unlucky in your culture.

In Like a Lion, Out Like a Lamb

> PREPARE TO READ

A. Look at the words (and phrases) in the list. Write the number(s) next to each word to show what you know. You may be able to write more than one number next to some of the words. You will study all of these words in this chapter.

1. I can use the word in a sentence.

2. I know <u>one meaning</u> of the word.

3. I know <u>more than one meaning</u> of the word.

4. I know how to pronounce the word.

B. Work with a partner. Look at the pictures. Do the activity and ask and answer the questions below.

1. Say each word in the list and point to the picture. If you don't know a word in English, ask your partner or look in your dictionary. Circle the words that are new to you.

cloud	lamb	lion	rainbow	sky	storm

2. Are there a lot of sayings (statements that many people believe) about the weather in your native language? What are they? Do you believe them?

_____ drop

_____ event

_____ guess

_____ hit

_____ in advance

_____ opposite

_____ predict

_____ storm

_____ superstition

_____ warning

C. Preview the Internet article "In Like a Lion, Out Like a Lamb." Then answer the question.

What do you think the title means?

> READ

Read "In Like a Lion, Out Like a Lamb." Underline the places in the reading where you find the answer for Exercise C.

---

http://www.superstitions/sayings.com

IN LIKE A LION, OUT LIKE A LAMB

1 Rainbow in the morning, shepherds[1] take **warning**. Rainbow at night, shepherd's delight.[2]

If March comes in like a lamb, it goes out like
5 a lion; if it comes in like a lion, it goes out like a lamb.

All languages and cultures have sayings about the weather. We often learn them as children. But are they fact or just
10 **superstition**? Let's see.

Saying 1: "Rainbow in the morning, shepherds take warning. Rainbow at night, shepherd's delight."

Fact or Superstition? FACT

15 Rainbows always appear **opposite** the sun. The sun rises in the east, so morning rainbows are always in the western sky. They appear when light from the rising sun **hits** small **drops** of water in a rain cloud in
20 the western sky. Most **storms** come out of the west. So a rainbow in the morning can mean rain is coming. What does an evening rainbow in the eastern sky mean? The rain has probably already passed.

25 Saying 2: "If March comes in like a lamb, it goes out like a lion; if it comes in like a lion, it goes out like a lamb."

Fact or Superstition? SUPERSTITION

This saying **predicts** the weather thirty days
30 **in advance**. If the weather is good (like a gentle[3] lamb) at the beginning of March, there will be stormy weather (like a roaring[4] lion) at the end. If you believe the saying, the opposite is also true. Stormy weather at the
35 beginning of the month means good weather at the end.

But you shouldn't believe it. In fact, you shouldn't believe most long-range[5] predictions about the weather. When one **event** happens
40 and a long time passes before the second event, your **guess** about the second event will be just that—a guess, not a fact.

Saying 1 is different. It predicts what will happen only in the next twelve to twenty-four
45 hours. When you base your prediction about tomorrow's weather on conditions you can see and feel today, there is a good chance that your prediction will be correct.

---

[1] **shepherd:** someone who takes care of sheep
[2] **delight:** great happiness or pleasure
[3] **gentle:** calm; not rough, loud, or forceful
[4] **roar:** make a deep, loud noise, like a lion
[5] **long-range:** relating to a time that continues far into the future

Vocabulary Check

Circle the letter of the correct answer to complete each sentence. The boldfaced words are the target words.

1. When you **guess**, you _____ the answer.
   a. imagine
   b. know
   c. think you know

2. A **drop** of water is a _____.
   a. glass
   b. little
   c. lot

3. If two houses are on **opposite** sides of a street, they are _____.
   a. far away from each other
   b. on different sides
   c. on the same side

4. _____ is an **event**.
   a. A wedding
   b. The weather
   c. The weekend

5. Wear your _____. There's going to be a **storm** later.
   a. dress
   b. suit
   c. raincoat

6. We can only **predict** events that are _____.
   a. important to us
   b. in the future
   c. in the past

7. There is a storm **warning**. The storm _____.
   a. already came
   b. is here
   c. might come

8. When you buy an airline ticket **in advance**, you _____.
   a. don't have the money to pay
   b. pay for it before you fly
   c. pay a lot less

9. When you believe in a **superstition**, you believe in _____.
   a. experience
   b. luck
   c. science

10. When sunlight **hits** a window, the window _____.
    a. appears
    b. gets dirty
    c. gets warm

> READ AGAIN

Read "In Like a Lion, Out Like a Lamb" again and complete the comprehension exercises on the next page. As you work, keep the reading goal in mind.

> 📖 **READING GOAL:** To decide whether sayings about the weather are fact or superstition

Comprehension Check

A. Check (✓) the statements that are true.

_____ **1.** Sayings about the weather are always false.

_____ **2.** Storms usually come out of the west.

_____ **3.** Evening rainbows appear only in the eastern sky.

_____ **4.** There is always bad weather at the beginning of March.

_____ **5.** It is possible to correctly predict what the weather will be like a month from today.

_____ **6.** If you want to predict the weather for the next day, you need to go outside and see and feel what is happening right now.

B. Which of the sayings are probably superstitions? Which might be facts? Write _S_ (superstition) or _F_ (fact). If you don't know a word in English, look in your dictionary.

_____ **1.** A wind from the south has rain in its mouth.

_____ **2.** Plant your beans when the moon is light. You will find that this is right.

_____ **3.** Red sky at morning, sailors take warning. Red sky at night, sailor's delight.

_____ **4.** Ring around the sun, time for fun. Ring around the moon, storm coming soon.

_____ **5.** If the groundhog (an animal that lives under the ground) sees its shadow on February 2, there will be another six weeks of winter.

_____ **6.** When squirrels (animals that live in trees) collect a lot of nuts, expect a hard winter.

C. Work with a partner. Compare and explain your answers for Exercise B. If you have different answers, decide who has the correct answer.

> DISCUSS

Work in small groups. Ask and answer the questions.

1. What sayings do you have about the weather in your culture? Translate them into English.

2. Which of your culture's weather sayings are probably superstitions? Which might be facts?

VOCABULARY SKILL BUILDING

Vocabulary Skill: Nouns that End in *-ing*

Some nouns end in *-ing*. These nouns are called *gerunds*. Don't confuse gerunds with verbs in the present participle form. They look similar, but one is a gerund and the other is a part of the verb. How can you tell?

-ing = noun

If the *-ing* word is the subject or object of a verb, it is a gerund.

EXAMPLE:

One famous <u>saying</u>   <u>is</u> about the month of March.
       ↓   ↓
    subject (gerund)   **verb**

All languages and cultures <u>have</u>   <u>sayings</u> about the weather.
              ↓   ↓
           verb   **object (gerund)**

Some verbs, such as *enjoy, finish,* and *keep,* are often followed by a gerund.

EXAMPLE:

I <u>enjoy</u>   <u>writing</u>.
 ↓   ↓
verb   **gerund**

-ing = verb

If the *-ing* word tells you what is happening (the action) and has a form of the verb *be* in front of it (*is, am, are, was, were,* or *been*), it is a verb.

EXAMPLE:

He   <u>is saying</u> something important.
↓   ↓
subject   **verb (action)**

Read the sentences and notice the boldfaced words. Are they gerunds (G) or verbs (V)? Check (✓) the correct column.

  G   **V**

_____   _____ **1.** I'm **warning** you—if you do it again, you'll be punished.

_____   _____ **2.** The teacher gave a **warning** to all of the students.

_____   _____ **3.** You should not hit another child. **Hitting** is never OK.

_____   _____ **4.** Mommy, Timmy is **hitting** me!

_____   _____ **5.** They didn't know the answer. They were **guessing**.

_____   _____ **6.** I dislike **guessing**. I like to know the answer.

The Superstitious Gene

> PREPARE TO READ

A. Look at the words in the list. Write the number(s) next to each word to show what you know. You may be able to write more than one number next to some of the words. You will study all of these words in this chapter.

1. I can use the word in a sentence.

2. I know <u>one meaning</u> of the word.

3. I know <u>more than one meaning</u> of the word.

4. I know how to pronounce the word.

B. Work with a partner. Look at the cartoon. Ask and answer the questions. If you don't know a word in English, ask your partner or look in your dictionary. Then write your new words on page 192.

1. How does the man feel? Why does he feel that way?

2. Superstitious people often change their behavior to avoid bad luck. Do you ever change your behavior because of a superstition?

_____ alive

_____ cause

_____ complete

_____ connect

_____ form

_____ hunt

_____ mind

_____ mirror

_____ nervous

_____ nonsense

Reading Skill: Understanding Cause and Effect

We often read to understand *why* something happens or is true. To understand why, you need to understand the relationship between *causes* and *effects*. The cause and effect may be in the same sentence or in different sentences. The cause may appear before or after the effect.

Look at the examples. The order of the words is different, but the relationship between the cause and the effect is the same.

EXAMPLE:

Rainbows appear when *sunlight hits drops of water in a cloud*.
↓   ↓
effect   **cause**

Sunlight hits drops of water in a cloud. Then *a rainbow appears*.
↓   ↓
cause   **effect**

C. Read the first paragraph of "The Superstitious Gene." Which set of sentences is an example of cause and effect from that paragraph? Check (✓) the answer.

_____ **1.** You are driving to a hotel. / A black cat crosses in front of your car.

_____ **2.** You get to the hotel. / Your room number is 1313.

_____ **3.** You hit a mirror with your suitcase. / The mirror breaks.

D. Preview the Internet article "The Superstitious Gene" on the next page. Then check (✓) the main topic.

_____ **1.** why so many people are superstitious

_____ **2.** why some people can predict the future

_____ **3.** why superstitious people are lucky

Read "The Superstitious Gene." As you read, pay attention to the causes and their effects.

http://www.superstitions.com/genes/

THE SUPERSTITIOUS GENE

1 Imagine this situation: You are driving to a hotel. A black cat crosses the street in front of your car. You get to the hotel. Your room number is 1313: room 13 on the 13th floor. When you go in

10 the room, you hit a **mirror** with your suitcase. The mirror breaks.

Can you predict what will happen next? Will this story have a happy ending? Most people will answer "No." But why? The only real

15 problem is the broken mirror. And that's not a very big problem. Then why does this story make many of us **nervous**?

The answer is human nature. In many cultures, people think that black cats,

20 the number 13, and broken mirrors are unlucky. And most people are at least a little superstitious.

It is easy to understand why people a long time ago were superstitious. They were trying

25 to understand the natural world. But today science can explain many things. Why are we still superstitious?

Kevin Foster, a biologist[1] at Harvard University, wants to find out. He thinks that

30 a belief in superstitions might be genetic.[2] To understand Foster's ideas, imagine this situation: It is thousands of years ago, and a man is **hunting** one morning. He sees a rainbow. Twelve hours later there is a bad

35 storm and he almost dies. He **connects** the rainbow and the storm in his **mind**. He **forms** a superstition: Morning rainbows **cause** storms. He tells his friends, but they don't believe in superstitions. The next time he

40 sees a morning rainbow, he is nervous. He warns his friends not to go out, but they don't listen. He stays home alone. His friends go out hunting and die in a bad storm.

The rainbow did not *cause* the storm. But

45 as you learned in Chapter 11, there *is* a real connection between rainbows and stormy weather. The superstitious hunter didn't understand *how* rainbows and stormy weather were connected, but his ability to

50 connect the two events helped him survive.

He has more experiences, he makes more connections, and he forms more superstitions. Most of his superstitions are **nonsense**. They don't help him, but they don't hurt him,

55 either. And because he survived that storm, he lives to have many children. He passes his superstitious genes[3] on to them. What about his unlucky friends? They weren't **alive** long enough to have children.

60 Foster's ideas are very new, and his studies are not **complete**. But he hopes that one day science will help us understand our superstitious nature.

---

[1] **biologist:** a person who studies living things

[2] **genetic:** relating to or caused by a gene (the part of a cell in a living thing that controls what the living thing is like)

[3] **gene:** a part of a cell in a living thing that controls how it develops

Vocabulary Check

Write the letter of the correct definition next to the word. Be careful.
There are two extra definitions.

_____ **1.** alive

_____ **2.** cause

_____ **3.** complete

_____ **4.** connect

_____ **5.** form

_____ **6.** hunt

_____ **7.** mind

_____ **8.** mirror

_____ **9.** nervous

_____ **10.** nonsense

a. your thoughts; your way of thinking

b. not feeling relaxed because you are afraid

c. a flat piece of glass that you can see yourself in

d. to find and kill animals for food

e. to join two or more things together

f. living; not dead

g. ideas or statements that are not true or that seem stupid

h. to imagine

i. to make

j. finished

k. a clear glass plate

l. to make something happen

> READ AGAIN

Read "The Superstitious Gene" again and complete the comprehension
exercises. As you work, keep the reading goal in mind.

> 📖 **READING GOAL:** To learn a possible reason why people are
> superstitious

Comprehension Check

A. Read the sentences from the reading. Write *cause* or *effect* above the
underlined parts of the sentences.

                                 cause   *effect*
_____   _____

1. When you go in the room, <u>you hit a mirror with your suitcase</u>. <u>The mirror

breaks</u>.

                                     _____

2. It is easy to understand why <u>people a long time ago were superstitious</u>.

                  _____

<u>They were trying to understand the natural world</u>.

3. He thinks that <u>a belief in superstitions</u> <u>might be genetic</u>.

_____   _____

4. <u>He connects the rainbow and the storm in his mind.</u> <u>He forms a superstition.</u>

_____   _____

5. The next time <u>he sees a morning rainbow,</u> <u>he is nervous.</u>

_____   _____

6. But <u>his ability to make the connection</u> <u>helped him survive.</u>

_____   _____

7. And because <u>he survived that storm,</u> <u>he lives to have many children.</u>

B. Complete the text with the words from the list. Try not to look back at the reading.

advantage	died	hunter	mind	survived
chance	events	hunting	rainbow	warned
connections	followed	imagine	storm	

People who are superstitious look for connections between

(1)_____. Their ability to make (2)_____ might

give them a survival (3)_____. How? To understand,

(4)_____ the following situation.

Thousands of years ago, there was a superstitious (5)_____ .

He always looked for connections between events. One day he saw a

morning rainbow. Twelve hours later there was a bad storm.

Because a bad storm (6)_____ the morning rainbow, the

man connected the rainbow and the (7)_____ in his

(8)_____. He said to himself, "In the future, I won't go

(9)_____ if a see a (10)_____ in the morning."

A week later he saw a morning rainbow, so he stayed home. He

(11) _____ his friends, but they didn't listen. They went out

(continued on next page)

hunting and (12)_____ in the storm. Because they died,

they didn't have the (13)_____ to have children.

Because the hunter was at home, he (14)_____ the

storm, and he lived long enough to have children.

C. **Work in pairs. Check your answers for Exercise C. Look back at the reading if necessary.**

> DISCUSS

Read the statements. Do you agree or disagree? Write a number for your opinion. Then talk in small groups. Explain your opinions.

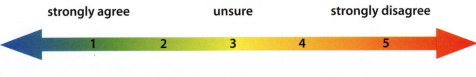

strongly agree	unsure	strongly disagree
1 2	3 4	5

_____ **a.** Kevin Foster's explanation is probably correct.

_____ **b.** Superstitions are nonsense.

_____ **c.** I believe in luck.

_____ **d.** I am lucky.

_____ **e.** People make their own luck.

Learn the Vocabulary

A. Find different forms of the words in the chart in your dictionary and complete the chart. Be careful. Sometimes two forms of the word have the same spelling.

Noun	Verb	Adjective
	connect	
		complete
hunter		
superstition		
	predict	predictable
		opposite
	form	
storm		

B. Complete the questions with the correct forms of the words in the chart on page 107. Be careful. You will not use all of the word forms.

1. Do you like to walk on the beach on _____ days?

2. When you meet someone for the first time, how long does it take you to _____ an opinion of him or her?

3. How long does it take you to _____ your homework every day?

4. Are you a(n) _____ person? For example, do you have a lucky number?

5. Do you think that some people can _____ the future?

6. Do your friends often _____ your decisions, or do they usually agree with you?

7. Do you use the Internet to _____ with old friends who live far away?

8. Which wild animal is the best _____?

C. Work with a partner. Check your answers for Exercise B. Then ask and answer the questions. Use the target words in your answers.

D. Make word cards for the new words in this unit. If a word has more than one form (for example, the words in the chart), list the different forms on the front of the card. Write the part of speech (for example *noun, verb, adjective*) next to each word. When you review those cards, try to remember all of the different forms of the word.

connect (verb)
connection (noun)

E. Go back to the vocabulary list at the beginning of each chapter. What did you learn about the target words? Add your numbers to the lists.

Vocabulary Practice 7, see page 199

> ## THINK BEFORE YOU READ

A. Work with a partner. Look at the picture. Ask and answer the questions. If you don't know a word in English, ask your partner or look in your dictionary. Then write your new words on page 192.

1. Where are the people in the picture? What is happening?

2. What are the people doing?

3. How do they feel?

B. Work with a partner. Ask and answer the questions.

1. Do you like to do things that are dangerous? For example, would you like to climb Mount Everest or jump out of an airplane?

2. Do you like to read stories about people who survive difficult situations? Why or why not?

3. Do you know a true survival story? Tell your group.

Trapped!

> PREPARE TO READ

A. Look at the words (and phrases) in the list. Write the number(s) next to each word to show what you know. You may be able to write more than one number next to some of the words. You will study all of these words in this chapter.

1. I can use the word in a sentence.

2. I know <u>one meaning</u> of the word.

3. I know <u>more than one meaning</u> of the word.

4. I know how to pronounce the word.

B. Work with a partner. Look at the picture. Ask and answer the questions. If you don't know a word in English, ask your partner or look in your dictionary. Then write your new words on page 192.

1. What kind of sport does the man in the picture do?

2. What is unusual about him?

3. What do you think happened to him?

_____ adventure

_____ experienced

_____ fall

_____ fear

_____ hold on

_____ realize

_____ recording

_____ risk

_____ thirst

_____ trapped

Reading Skill: Using Details to Visualize a Story

When you read, it is helpful to visualize, or make a picture in your head of what the writer is describing. In a narrative (a story about something that happened), the writer uses details to make the story more interesting. Pay attention to the details. Use them to help you visualize what is happening.

C. Scan the magazine article "Trapped!" on the next page for details. Then complete the sentences.

1. The story is about a rock climber named _____.

2. A rock fell on his _____.

3. The rock weighed _____.

4. He had _____ of water.

5. He was trapped for _____ days.

6. He cut off his arm with _____.

7. He had to climb _____ to the bottom of the canyon.

8. He had to walk _____ to find help.

9. In 2008, he climbed _____.

Read "Trapped!" Underline the most interesting details.

Trapped!

1   On a beautiful April day, Aron Ralston decided to go rock climbing alone. Ralston was an **experienced** climber, and it was not unusual for him to climb alone. But for the first time in his
5   life, Ralston did not tell anyone where he was going. That decision almost cost him his life.[1]

The day started out fine. Ralston went to a canyon[2] miles away from the nearest town. The climbing was not very difficult,
10   and the weather was beautiful. But in rock climbing, there is always the danger that a rock will **fall** on you. On that beautiful spring day, it happened to Ralston. An 800-pound (363-kilogram) rock fell on his right hand.
15   Ralston's first thought was about his hand. It hurt a lot. But soon he **realized** that he had much bigger problems. His arm was **trapped** under the rock. He had less than a liter of water and almost no food. And nobody knew
20   where he was.

For five days, Ralston experienced **thirst**, hunger, and **fear**. He used his camcorder[3] to make a **recording** for his family. "I'm sorry," he told them. "I go out looking for **adventure**
25   and **risk** so I can feel alive. But ... I don't tell someone where I'm going—that's just dumb."[4] On the fifth day, he said good-bye. "I'm **holding on**, but it's really slowing down, the time is going really slow. So again, love to
30   everyone ... Thank you. I love you."

On the sixth day, Ralston knew that he was close to death. His only hope? To cut off the bottom of his right arm. It might sound unbelievable, but in fact, he used a
35   $15 pocketknife to do just that. But Ralston's survival story does not end there. He wasn't trapped anymore, but he was still alone in the canyon, miles away from help. First he had to climb down 60 feet (18.3 meters) to the
40   bottom of the canyon. Then he had to walk six miles before he found help.

Ralston knows that he was lucky to survive. He now has a prosthetic arm and continues to climb. In June 2008, he climbed 20,320-
45   foot (6,194-meter) Mount Denali in Alaska (the northernmost U.S. state)—alone. But his experience in that canyon taught him an important lesson. He still climbs alone, but he always tells someone where he is going.

---

[1] **cost him his life:** make someone lose his life

[2] **canyon:** a deep valley with very steep sides

[3] **camcorder:** a type of camera that you use to record pictures and sound onto videotape

[4] **dumb:** stupid

Vocabulary Check

Look at the pictures and read the definitions. Write the boldfaced word from the reading next to the correct picture or definition. Use the correct form of the word.

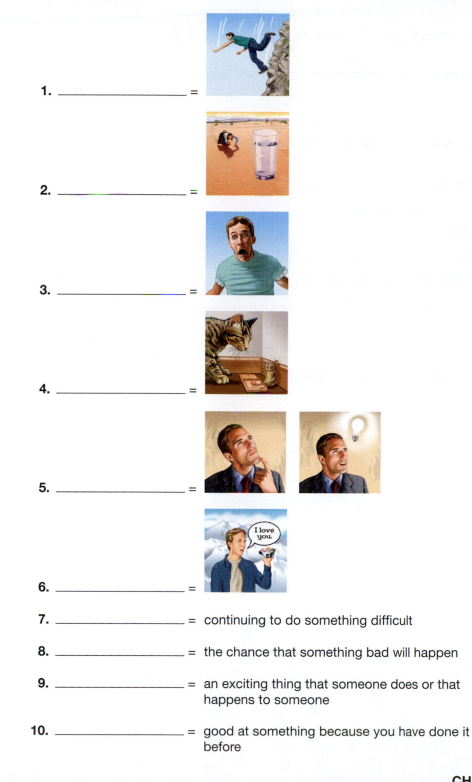

1. _____ =

2. _____ =

3. _____ =

4. _____ =

5. _____ =

6. _____ =

7. _____ = continuing to do something difficult

8. _____ = the chance that something bad will happen

9. _____ = an exciting thing that someone does or that happens to someone

10. _____ = good at something because you have done it before

▶ READ AGAIN

Read "Trapped!" again and complete the comprehension exercises. As you work, keep the reading goal in mind.

> 📖 **READING GOAL:** To retell Aron Ralston's survival story and include the most important details

Comprehension Check

A. Answer as many questions as you can without looking back at the reading.

1. Where was Ralston on the day he got hurt? What kind of day was it?

   _____

2. What was Ralston's mistake?

   _____

3. How did he get trapped? How long was he trapped?

   _____

4. Why did he make a recording?

   _____

5. What did he decide to do? What kind of knife did he use?

   _____

6. How far did he have to walk before he found help?

   _____

7. What did he do in 2008?

   _____

B. Look back at the reading and check your answers for Exercise A.

C. Work in small groups. Sit in a circle. You are going to tell Ralston's story. One student will start and say one or two sentences. The next student will continue the story, and so on. Include as many details as you can. If someone makes a mistake, correct it before continuing the story. Do not look back at the reading.

> DISCUSS

Work in small groups. Which of the words in the list describe Aron Ralston? Explain your answers with details from the reading.

adventurous	clever	foolish	lucky	powerful
a risk-taker	emotional	fun	nervous	responsible
ashamed	famous	intelligent	practical	serious

Why Do Some Survive?

> PREPARE TO READ

A. Look at the words in the list. Write the number(s) next to each word to show what you know. You may be able to write more than one number next to some of the words. You will study all of these words in this chapter.

1. I can use the word in a sentence.

2. I know <u>one meaning</u> of the word.

3. I know <u>more than one meaning</u> of the word.

4. I know how to pronounce the word.

B. Work with a partner. Look at the picture. Ask and answer the questions. If you don't know a word in English, ask your partner or look in your dictionary. Then write your new words on page 192.

1. What is the story behind the picture? That is, what do you think happened?

2. Do you think the people survived? Why or why not?

_____ community

_____ crash

_____ disaster

_____ independent

_____ instead

_____ limit

_____ security

_____ senses

_____ skilled

_____ trust

Reading Skill: Making a Graphic Organizer

To understand how the ideas in a reading are related to each other, it can help to make a *graphic organizer*.

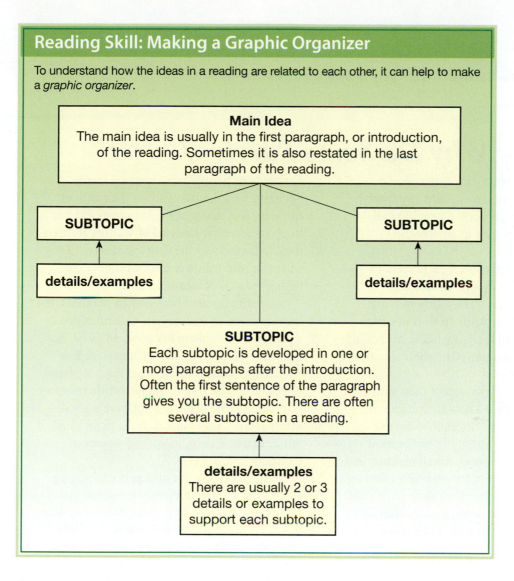

Main Idea
The main idea is usually in the first paragraph, or introduction, of the reading. Sometimes it is also restated in the last paragraph of the reading.

SUBTOPIC

SUBTOPIC

details/examples

details/examples

SUBTOPIC
Each subtopic is developed in one or more paragraphs after the introduction. Often the first sentence of the paragraph gives you the subtopic. There are often several subtopics in a reading.

details/examples
There are usually 2 or 3 details or examples to support each subtopic.

C. Preview the newspaper book review "Why Do Some Survive?" on the next page. Then answer the questions.

1. What is the main idea? Check (✓) the answer.

_____ **a.** Seventy-five percent of people in a disaster don't accept what is happening to them.

_____ **b.** Disaster survivors accept what is happening to them very quickly.

_____ **c.** Disaster survivors are often independent thinkers.

_____ **d.** Disaster survivors listen to themselves.

_____ **e.** Disaster survivors have strong connections to friends and family.

_____ **f.** Disaster survivors share characteristics that help them survive.

2. How many subtopics are there? _____

READ

Read "Why Do Some Survive?" Were your answers for Exercise C correct?

Why Do Some Survive?

1   In almost every **disaster**, some people survive. Do these survivors share any special characteristics? In his book *Deep Survival*, Laurence Gonzales tries to answer that
5 question.

     Gonzales says that about 75 percent of people in a disaster do one of two things. Some of them freeze.[1] They stop moving and thinking. Others walk around in a daze.[2]
10 They don't seem to realize what is happening. And when they do understand their situation, they won't accept it.

     But disaster survivors accept their situation very quickly, and they know their own
15 **limits**, Gonzales says. Often, they are not the most **skilled**, the strongest, or the most experienced in their group. Small children and inexperienced climbers, for example, often survive in the wild better than stronger people
20 do. Why? They know when to rest. They know when they should be fearful. They **trust** their **senses**.

     Many survivors are also **independent** thinkers. When planes **crashed** into the
25 World Trade Center on September 11, 2001, hundreds of people were trapped inside. **Security** told them to wait in their offices for help. But many of the survivors did not listen to security. **Instead** of waiting for help,
30 they walked down the stairs to safety. "They were not rule followers; they thought for themselves …" Gonzales says.

     Survivors do not always listen to others, but they do listen to themselves. Gonzales gives
35 a personal example in his book. In 1979, his boss asked him to fly from Chicago to Los Angeles. Gonzales asked what kind of plane it was. When he found out, he decided not to go. That type of plane did not have a good
40 safety record. Later that day, the plane crashed. All 271 people died, including several of Gonzales's coworkers.

     Many survivors are also part of a strong **community**. They feel very connected to
45 family and friends, says Gonzales. They want to see them again. Aron Ralston, the climber who cut off his own arm, is a good example. Thinking about his family helped him hold on. And sometimes to survive, you just need
50 to hold on a little longer.

---

[1] **freeze:** suddenly stop moving and stay very quiet and still

[2] **in a daze:** unable to think clearly

Vocabulary Check

Write *T* (true) or *F* (false) for each statement. Then correct the false statements to make them true. The boldfaced words are the target words.

_____*F*_____ **1.** You should ^*not* **trust** people who lie to you.

_____*F*_____ **2.** When you buy one book **instead** of another book, you buy ~~both~~ *one* books.

_____ **3.** An earthquake is a natural **disaster**.

_____ **4.** If you trust your **senses**, you'll leave if you feel uncomfortable somewhere.

_____ **5.** When you belong to a **community**, you are a part of a group of people.

_____ **6.** People who work in **security** are responsible for the safety of other people, places, and things.

_____ **7.** An **independent** person needs a lot of help from other people.

_____ **8.** To become a **skilled** mountain climber, you need to climb a lot of mountains.

_____ **9.** When a plane **crashes**, it lands safely.

_____ **10.** You cannot buy a $2,000 sofa with a credit card that has a $1,500 **limit**.

> READ AGAIN

Read "Why Do Some Survive?" again and complete the comprehension exercises on the next page. As you work, keep the reading goal in mind.

> **READING GOAL:** To understand the characteristics that help some people survive a disaster

Comprehension Check

A. Complete the graphic organizer of the reading.

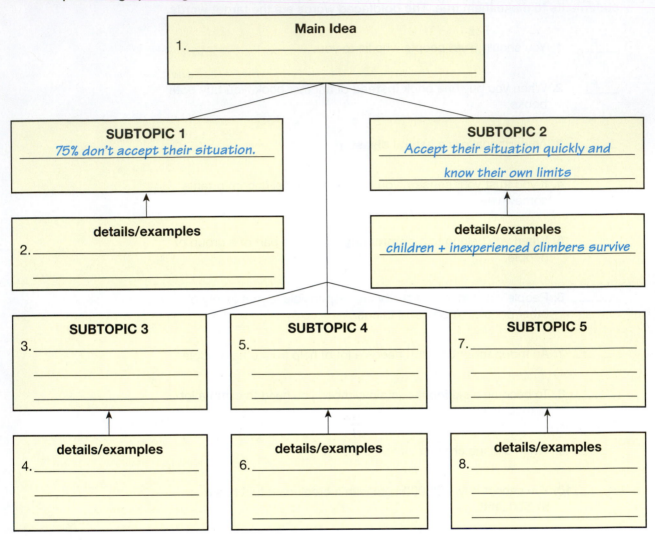

Main Idea

1. _____

_____

SUBTOPIC 1

75% don't accept their situation.

details/examples

2. _____

_____

SUBTOPIC 2

Accept their situation quickly and

know their own limits

details/examples

children + inexperienced climbers survive

SUBTOPIC 3

3. _____

_____

_____

details/examples

4. _____

_____

_____

SUBTOPIC 4

5. _____

_____

_____

details/examples

6. _____

_____

_____

SUBTOPIC 5

7. _____

_____

_____

details/examples

8. _____

_____

_____

B. Read the descriptions. Who has the best chance of surviving a disaster?
Circle the name of the person.

1. **Sara** loves her husband very much. They are very happy together. He
   makes most of the decisions for the family.

2. **Amy** is independent and intelligent. She has a good job. She does not
   have any close friends. She sees her family once or twice a year.

3. **Sam** is tall, healthy, and very strong. He does not fear anything. When he
   is hurt or sick, he doesn't tell anyone. He doesn't like to ask for help.

4. **Peter** has a lot of close friends. He has a good relationship with his
   parents, but he lives alone. He trusts his own feelings.

C. Work in small groups. Compare and explain your answers for Exercise B.

> VOCABULARY SKILL BUILDING

Vocabulary Skill: The Prefix in-

In Chapter 10, you learned that the prefix *dis-* means *not*. The prefix *in-* can also mean *not* when it is added to some adjectives. It gives the adjective the opposite meaning.

EXAMPLE:

independent = not dependent

A. Add the prefix *in-* to make new words.

1. dependent _____*independent*_____   4. active _____

2. experienced _____   5. offensive _____

3. complete _____   6. efficient _____

B. Complete the sentences with the words from Exercise A. Be careful. You will use only one form of each word.

1. Your homework is _____. Please finish it.

2. You are too _____. If you want to lose weight, you must exercise.

3. Her behavior was _____. I don't understand why you are angry at her.

4. Computers are more _____ at some things than people are. For example, they can add numbers much faster.

5. He didn't get the job because he was _____. They wanted someone with more training.

6. She lives alone, without the help of anyone in her family or community. She is completely _____.

> DISCUSS

Work in small groups. Ask and answer the questions.

1. Which characteristics of a survivor do you have? Which don't you have?

2. How do you think you would behave in a disaster?

3. Would you like to read Gonzales's book? Why or why not?

Learn the Vocabulary

A. Read the sentences. Figure out the meanings of the boldfaced words. Underline the words that help you understand the meaning.

1. Gonzales says that about 75 percent of people in a disaster do one of two things. Some of them **freeze**. <u>They stop moving and thinking</u>.

   Freeze means *to stop moving and thinking*.

2. Others walk around **in a daze**. They don't seem to realize what is happening. And when they do understand their situation, they won't accept it.

   In a daze means _____.

3. "I'm sorry," he told them. "I go out looking for adventure and risk so <u>I can feel alive</u>. <u>But . . . I don't tell someone where I'm going</u>—that's just dumb."

   Dumb means *something bad*.

4. Rainbow in the morning, shepherds take warning. Rainbow at night, shepherd's **delight**.

   Delight means _____.

5. This saying predicts the weather thirty days in advance: *If the weather is good (like a* **gentle** *lamb) at the beginning of March, there will be stormy weather (like a* **roaring** *lion) at the end*. If you believe the saying, the opposite is also true. Stormy weather at the beginning of the month means good weather at the end.

Gentle means _____.

Roaring means _____.

B. Look up the meanings of the words from Exercise A in your dictionary. Copy the definition that fits the context. Compare the dictionary definition to the definitions you wrote. Are they similar?

1. freeze: _____

2. in a daze: _____

3. dumb: _____

4. delight: _____

5. gentle: _____

6. roar: _____

C. Make cards for the new words in this unit. Include the words from Exercise B and the words you wrote on page 192.

D. Go back to the vocabulary list at the beginning of each chapter. What did you learn about the target words? Add your numbers to the lists.

Vocabulary Practice 8, see page 200

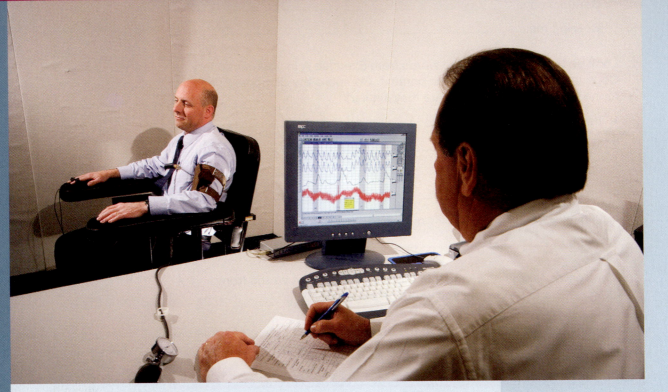

> THINK BEFORE YOU READ

A. Work with a partner. Look at the picture. Ask and answer the questions. If you don't know a word in English, ask your partner or look in your dictionary. Then write your new words on page 192.

   1. Where are the people in the picture?

   2. What are they doing?

B. Work with a partner. Ask and answer the questions.

   1. Do you believe that lie detector tests really work? That is, do they show whether or not someone is lying? Can you trust the results?

   2. How can you tell when someone is lying?

   3. Is lying always wrong? Are there any "good" lies?

Do Animals Lie?

> PREPARE TO READ

A. Look at the words in the list. Write the number(s) next to each word to show what you know. You may be able to write more than one number next to some of the words. You will study all of these words in this chapter.

1. I can use the word in a sentence.

2. I know <u>one meaning</u> of the word.

3. I know <u>more than one meaning</u> of the word.

4. I know how to pronounce the word.

B. Work with a partner. Look at the picture. Ask and answer the questions. If you don't know a word in English, ask your partner or look in your dictionary. Then write your new words on page 192.

1. What is happening in the picture?

2. Do you think that animals lie? Explain your answer.

_____ adoptive

_____ bury

_____ expert

_____ fool

_____ nest

_____ pretend

_____ sneak

_____ steal

_____ successful

_____ thief

To check your understanding of a reading, it can be helpful to write a *summary* of it. A summary is much shorter than the reading. It includes only the main idea, the subtopics that support the main idea, and just the most important examples or details that support the subtopics.

C. Preview the magazine article "Do Animals Lie?" Then check (✓) the main idea.

_____ **1.** Birds are very good at fooling other animals.

_____ **2.** Birds and chimpanzees behave in strange ways.

_____ **3.** Animals sometimes act dishonestly in order to survive.

_____ **4.** Chimpanzees know how to lie.

> READ

Read "Do Animals Lie?" Was your answer for Exercise C correct?

Do Animals Lie?

1 　　Most people agree that honesty is a good thing. But does Mother Nature agree? Animals can't talk, but can they lie in other ways? Can they lie with their bodies and behavior? Animal
5 **experts** may not call it lying, but they do agree that many animals, from birds to chimpanzees, behave dishonestly to **fool** other animals. Why? Dishonesty often helps them survive.

　　Many kinds of birds are very **successful**
10 at fooling other animals. For example, a bird called the plover sometimes **pretends** to be hurt in order to protect its young. When a predator[1] gets close to its **nest**, the plover leads the predator away from the nest. How? It
15 pretends to have a broken wing.[2] The predator follows the "hurt" adult, leaving the baby birds safe in the nest.

　　Another kind of bird, the scrub
20 jay, **buries** its food so it always has something to eat. Scrub jays are also **thieves**. They
25 watch where others bury their food and **steal** it. But clever scrub jays seem to know when a thief is watching them. So they go back later, unbury
30 the food, and bury it again somewhere else.

　　Birds called cuckoos have found a way to have babies without doing much work. How? They don't make nests. Instead, they **sneak** into other birds' nests. Then they lay[3] their

---

[1] **predator:** an animal that kills and eats other animals
[2] **wing:** the part of a bird's body used for flying
[3] **lay:** make eggs come out of the body

35 eggs and fly away. When the baby birds hatch,[4] their **adoptive** parents feed them.

Chimpanzees, or chimps, can also be sneaky. After a fight, the losing chimp will give its hand to the other. When the winning chimp
40 puts out its hand, too, the chimps are friendly again. But an animal expert once saw a losing chimp take the winner's hand and start fighting again.

Chimps are sneaky in other ways, too.
45 When chimps find food that they love, such as bananas, it is natural for them to cry out. Then other chimps come running. But some clever chimps learn to cry very softly when they find food. That way, other chimps don't hear them,
50 and they don't need to share their food.

As children, many of us learn the saying "You can't fool Mother Nature." But maybe you can't trust her, either.

---

[4] **hatch:** be born by coming out of an egg

Vocabulary Check

Write the letter of the correct definition next to the word. Be careful. There are two extra definitions.

_____ 1. adoptive

_____ 2. bury

_____ 3. expert

_____ 4. fool

_____ 5. nest

_____ 6. pretend

_____ 7. sneak

_____ 8. steal

_____ 9. successful

_____ 10. thief

a. to put something in the ground and cover it with dirt

b. to trick someone

c. to do something quietly because you do not want people to see or hear you

d. someone who steals something

e. to hurt someone or something

f. responsible

g. a person with special skill or knowledge in a subject

h. a place made by a bird to live in

i. to behave as if something is true when you know that it is not

j. to take something that you do not own without asking for it

k. doing well

l. (parents) not by birth but by taking a child that is not your own into your family and raising it as your own

> READ AGAIN

Read "Do Animals Lie?" again and complete the comprehension exercises. As you read, keep the reading goal in mind.

> 📖 **READING GOAL:** To complete a summary of "Do Animals Lie?"

Comprehension Check

A. Read the sentences about the reading. Write *MI* for main idea, *ST* for subtopics, or *EX* for example.

_____ 1. Animal experts may not call it lying, but they do agree that many animals, from birds to chimpanzees, behave dishonestly to fool other animals.

_____ 2. Many kinds of birds are very successful at fooling other animals.

_____ 3. Clever scrub jays know when a thief is watching them bury food. So they go back later, unbury the food, and bury it again somewhere else.

_____ 4. Cuckoos have found a way to have babies without doing much work.

_____ 5. Chimpanzees can also be sneaky.

_____ 6. A loser chimp took the winner's hand and started fighting again.

_____ 7. Some clever chimps learn to cry very softly when they find food.

B. Complete the graphic organizer with information from the reading.

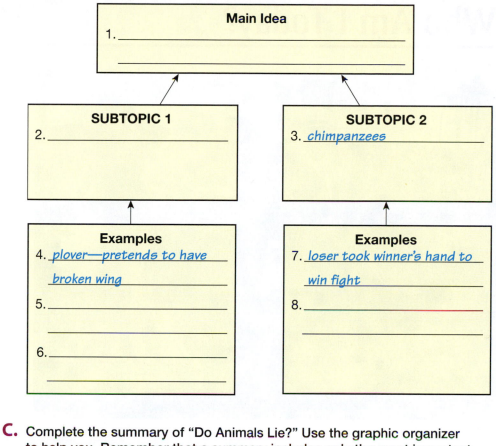

Main Idea

1. _____

_____

SUBTOPIC 1

2. _____

SUBTOPIC 2

3. _chimpanzees_____

Examples

4. _plover—pretends to have_

_broken wing_____

5. _____

_____

6. _____

_____

Examples

7. _loser took winner's hand to_

_win fight_____

8. _____

C. Complete the summary of "Do Animals Lie?" Use the graphic organizer to help you. Remember that a summary includes only the most important details or examples. When you finish, compare your summary to a classmate's.

Sometimes, animals _____. Why? It helps them

_____. _____ are very good at

_____. For example, _____.

Chimpanzees also _____.

For example, _____.

> DISCUSS

Work in small groups. Ask and answer the questions.

1. Which emotions do you think animals feel? Circle them.

    ashamed   fearful   nervous   offended   surprised

2. How do these animals show the emotions that you circled in item 1?

    birds   chimpanzees   horses   cats   dogs

Who Am I Today?

> PREPARE TO READ

A. Look at the words (and phrases) in the list. Write the number(s) next to each word to show what you know. You may be able to write more than one number next to some of the words. You will study all of these words in this chapter.

1. I can use the word in a sentence.

2. I know <u>one meaning</u> of the word.

3. I know <u>more than one meaning</u> of the word.

4. I know how to pronounce the word.

B. Work with a partner. Look at the picture. Ask and answer the questions. If you don't know a word in English, ask your partner or look in your dictionary. Then write your new words on page 192.

1. Who is the actor in the photograph?

2. What is the name of the movie that the photograph comes from? What is the movie about? (If you don't know, guess.)

_____ career

_____ cash

_____ condition

_____ crime

_____ financial

_____ identity

_____ lawyer

_____ professional

_____ release

_____ run away

C. Preview "Who Am I Today?" Then check (✓) the questions that you think the reading will answer.

_____ **1.** Why is Frank Abagnale famous?

_____ **2.** How many children does Frank Abagnale have?

_____ **3.** What is a confidence man?

_____ **4.** How many confidence men are there in the world?

_____ **5.** How many careers has Frank Abagnale had?

_____ **6.** What are prisons in France like?

> READ

Read "Who Am I Today?" Underline the answers to the questions that you checked (✓) for Exercise C.

❧ Who Am I Today? ❧

1   Today Frank W. Abagnale works with governments, banks, and other businesses. He helps protect them from **financial crime**. In fact, he is a leading expert on financial crime.

       But this is not Abagnale's first **career**. Before his twenty-second birthday, he
5   had tried being a doctor, a college professor, an airline pilot,[1] and a **lawyer**. And he did all of it without any **professional** training. How? Abagnale was a confidence man (or a con man).

       Confidence men get people to trust them. Then they steal their money. Abagnale was one of the most successful confidence men in U.S. history. Between
10   the ages of sixteen and twenty-one, Abagnale **cashed** $2.5 million in fraudulent[2] checks. He fooled people in every state in the United States and in twenty-six other countries, too.

       Abagnale's life as a confidence man began when he **ran away** from home. He was sixteen. He arrived in New York City with only $100 in his pocket. He added
15   ten years to his birthdate on his driver's license so that he could get a job.

       Over the next five years, Abagnale pretended to be a pilot. He traveled all over the world for free. He pretended to be a doctor and worked at a hospital. He pretended to be a college professor and taught courses at a university. He never went to law school, but he passed the exam to become a lawyer and worked in a
20   law office.

       Abagnale made some money from his jobs, but he got rich from his real work: making and cashing bad checks. Bankers trusted him. Why? He pretended to be a professional, and they believed him. When someone started to suspect[3] him, he moved to a new city or country. There he began a new life with a new **identity**.

(continued on next page)

---

[1] **pilot:** someone who flies an aircraft

[2] **fraudulent:** intended to deceive people

[3] **suspect:** think that someone may be guilty of a crime

25   The police finally caught Abagnale in France, and he went to prison.[4] He was only twenty-one years old. At first he was in a French prison, but later he was moved to the United States. After five years, the U.S. government agreed to **release** him, but with one **condition**. He had to work without pay for the FBI. His job? To help them fight financial crime.

30   For the past thirty years, that is what Abagnale has done. Years ago, he also paid back the $2.5 million that he stole. He continues to help the FBI today, and he never takes any money for his work.

    Abagnale wrote about his life in the book *Catch Me if You Can*. In 2002, the book became a movie, with Leonardo DiCaprio as Abagnale.

---

[4] **prison:** a large building where people are kept as a punishment for a crime

Vocabulary Check

Circle the letter of the correct answer to complete each sentence. The boldfaced words are the target words.

1. When you **cash** a check you _____.
   - **a.** pay a bill
   - **b.** get money
   - **c.** steal money

2. _____ is a **career**.
   - **a.** Teaching
   - **b.** Studying
   - **c.** Having children

3. _____ is a **crime**.
   - **a.** Trusting people
   - **b.** Stealing
   - **c.** Working for free

4. _____ is serious. He will need a good **lawyer**.
   - **a.** His crime
   - **b.** His illness
   - **c.** The storm

5. _____ is a **financial** crime.
   - **a.** Cashing a check
   - **b.** Running away
   - **c.** Stealing money

6. To change your **identity**, first you need to _____.
   - **a.** cash a check
   - **b.** change your name
   - **c.** start a career

7. Being a **professional** tennis player is a _____.
   - **a.** career
   - **b.** hobby
   - **c.** skill

8. I go fishing for _____. When I catch a fish, I **release** it.
   - **a.** food
   - **b.** fun
   - **c.** survival

9. If you **run away** from a police officer, he or she will _____ you.
   - **a.** follow
   - **b.** identify
   - **c.** release

10. The police will release him if he _____. That's their **condition**.
    - **a.** is a criminal
    - **b.** has a career
    - **c.** tells the truth

READ AGAIN

Read "Who Am I Today?" again and complete the comprehension exercises. As you work, keep the reading goal in mind.

> 📖 **READING GOAL:** To understand Abagnale's story and make guesses about his life and experiences

Comprehension Check

A. Circle the letter of the correct answer to complete each sentence. There is only one correct answer.

1. Abagnale got rich from _____.
   a. cashing bad checks
   b. his jobs as a pilot, a doctor, a lawyer, and a professor
   c. working with the FBI

2. From the ages of sixteen to twenty-one, Abagnale's real career was as _____.
   a. a banker
   b. a confidence man
   c. an FBI agent

3. Abagnale was able to fool bankers because they thought _____.
   a. he worked for the FBI
   b. he was a professional and trusted him
   c. he had a new identity

4. Abagnale learned a lot about financial crime _____.
   a. as a confidence man
   b. in college
   c. when he studied to be a lawyer

5. Today, Abagnale is _____.
   a. a confidence man
   b. an expert on financial crime
   c. the leader of the FBI

6. Abagnale still _____ the FBI.
   a. gives money to
   b. helps
   c. gets money for his work with

B. Work with a partner. Read the questions and underline the answers in the reading. If you do not find an answer, write *?* next to the question.

1. Why did Abagnale run away from home?

2. How old was Abagnale when he became a con man?

3. Did Abagnale hurt anyone when he pretended to be a doctor?

4. Did Abagnale ever fly an airplane when he pretended to be a pilot?

5. Did Abagnale teach any classes when he pretended to be a professor?

6. What was Abagnale doing in France before the police caught him?

C. Work with a partner. Which questions in Exercise B couldn't you answer? Use your imagination to guess the answers. Then share your answers with the class and explain them.

D. Find the real answers to the questions in Exercise C. You can find them in the book *Catch Me if You Can* or in the movie.

> DISCUSS

Work in small groups. Ask and answer the questions.

1. What is the meaning of the title of the reading "Who Am I Today?"

2. Which kind of professional is the easiest to pretend to be—an airline pilot, a doctor, a lawyer, or a professor? Which is the most difficult to pretend to be?

3. Do you think that the FBI did the right thing when they released Abagnale from prison? Why or why not?

> VOCABULARY SKILL BUILDING

Vocabulary Skill: The Prefix *un-*

Like the prefixes *dis-* and *in-*, the prefix *un-* means *not*.
When *un-* is added to an **adjective**, it gives the word the opposite meaning.

EXAMPLE:

unprofessional = not professional

When *un-* is added to a **verb**, it means to *undo* an action done before.

EXAMPLE:

The bird unburies the food. = First a bird buries the food. Then it *undoes* the action of burying the food and removes it from the ground.

A. Are the words adjectives or verbs? Write *A* or *V*.

_____V_____ **1.** unbury   _____ **7.** unlock

_____ **2.** uncover   _____ **8.** unpack

_____ **3.** undress   _____ **9.** unsafe

_____ **4.** unconditional   _____ **10.** unskilled

_____ **5.** unemotional   _____ **11.** unsuccessful

_____ **6.** unhealthy   _____ **12.** unnatural

B. Write the words from Exercise A next to their definitions.

1. remove from under the ground   = _____

2. not good for you   = _____

3. remove the top of something   = _____

4. remove one's clothes   = _____

5. open with a key   = _____

6. with no limits or conditions   = _____

7. with no training or special ability = _____

8. losing or not doing well   = _____

9. dangerous   = _____

10. not showing one's feelings   = _____

11. remove from a suitcase   = _____

12. not normal or usual   = _____

Learn the Vocabulary

Using Word Parts to Guess Meaning

For words that contain word parts such as prefixes (*dis-, in-, un-*, etc.), you can use the <u>word part meaning</u> together with the <u>context</u> to make a <u>definition</u> of the new word.

EXAMPLE:

*That cereal wasn't popular, so the company **dis**continued it.*

Word Part Meaning:

***dis**- = not*

Context:
Who discontinued it? *The company did.*
Why did the company discontinue it? *The cereal wasn't popular.*

Definition:
When a company **discontinues** something, it *stops making it* because not enough people buy it.

You can check your definition by replacing the new word in the sentence with the definition. If the sentence doesn't make sense, then your definition is probably not correct.

EXAMPLE:

The cereal wasn't popular, so the company <u>stopped making</u> it.

Be careful. Sometimes a word looks like it has a prefix, when in fact the letters are just a part of the spelling of the word. For example, the word *discontinue* has a prefix, but the word *distance* does not.

A. Circle the word in each group of words that does <u>not</u> contain a prefix.

1. disability   discuss   dishonest

2. under   unimaginable   unlimited

3. incorrect   indecision   information

B. Write a definition for each boldfaced word. Use the strategy on page 136.

1. He has a serious physical **disability**. He can't walk.

   Definition of **disability**: _____

2. For only $20 a month, you get **unlimited** calls at night and on weekends.

   Definition of **unlimited**: _____

3. Because of your **indecision**, we lost our chance to buy that house.

   Definition of **indecision**: _____

C. Now find the words from Exercise B in your dictionary and check your definitions.

D. Go back to the vocabulary list at the beginning of each chapter. What did you learn about the target words? Add your numbers to the lists.

Vocabulary Practice 9, see page 201

FLUENCY PRACTICE 3

> READING 1

Before You Read

Scan the home page of Dan Jackson's blog on the next page and answer the questions.

1. What is Dan Jackson's profession?

_____

2. Why hasn't he posted anything in a long time?

_____

3. What is his new project?

_____

4. Who does he need help from?

_____

Read

A. Read Dan Jackson's blog. Time yourself. Write your start and end times and your total reading time. Then calculate your reading speed (words per minute) and write it in the progress chart on page 205.

Start time: _____   **End time:** _____   **Total time:** _____ (in seconds)

Reading speed:
257 words ÷ _____ (total time in seconds) x 60 = _____ words per minute

---

http://www.blog.com/danjackson/

Adventures in English with Dan Jackson

1   Hi, there. First of all, I want to apologize for not posting anything for so long. But I know you will understand when you hear about my adventures. I've been traveling all over the United States to learn about superstitions in different parts of the country. Follow the link on the right to read about it.
5   When you finish reading, make sure you return here. I have a great new project, but I can't do it without your help.

The project: A collection of superstitions from all over the world
All cultures have superstitions. Some superstitions are specific to one culture, country, or even community. There are also superstitions that are
10 the same in many cultures.

Some people really believe in superstitions. Others don't believe but follow certain superstitions anyway.   And other people think that superstitions are complete nonsense. But in my experience, even the least superstitious people like to learn about superstitions.

15 So…here's my idea. I am asking you to post information on superstitions in your country on my website. I will collect the information you give me and put it in a book. I already have a publisher for the project. Any money from the book will go to an organization that works to form better understanding among cultures.

20 The people who send in information—that's you!—will help me decide which organization will get the money. And if I use what you write, your name will appear in the book. So…let's go! Send me a post with your country's superstitions. And thanks in advance for your help!

http://www.
superstitionsinamerica.
com

Dan Jackson, an English teacher who loves to travel and learn about other cultures

---

B. Read Dan Jackson's blog again, a little faster this time. Write your start and end times and your total reading time. Then calculate your reading speed (words per minute) and write it in the progress chart on page 205.

Start time: _____   **End time:** _____   **Total time:** _____ (in seconds)

Reading speed:
257 words ÷ _____ (total time in seconds) x 60 = _____ words per minute

Comprehension Check

A. Circle the letter of the correct answer to complete each sentence.

1. The purpose of Dan Jackson's blog is to _____.
   a. share information about other cultures
   b. find American students
   c. give people travel ideas

2. Dan recently traveled around the United States to _____.
   a. teach people about superstitions in other cultures
   b. learn about superstitions in different parts of the country
   c. find out if superstitions are really true

3. Dan plans to write _____.
   a. a blog about superstitions around the world
   b. a book about superstitions in different cultures
   c. a book about superstitions in the United States

4. Most of the readers of Dan's blog are probably _____.
   a. business owners who want to sell things in other countries
   b. people who want to practice their English and learn about other cultures
   c. teachers who already know a lot about many different cultures

5. Dan plans to use the money from the sale of his book to _____.
   a. give money to an organization that does work on cultural understanding
   b. pay the people who send him information about superstitions in their cultures
   c. form an organization that will help people from different cultures understand each other

B. Complete the summary of Dan Jackson's blog. You will need to write more than one word in the spaces.

Dan Jackson is a(n) (1)_____. He is interested in

(2)_____. His new project is (3)_____.

He wants the readers of his blog to (4)_____.

He plans to (5)_____ and put them in a book. He

already has a (6)_____ for the book. If the book is a

financial success, Dan will (7)_____.

C. Check your answers for the comprehension questions in the Answer Key on page 206. Then calculate your score and write it in the progress chart on page 205.

_____ (my number correct) ÷ 12 x 100 = _____%

> READING 2

Before You Read

Scan the blog posts on the next page and answer the questions.

1. Which countries do the people who have posted comments come from?

   _____

2. How did Sungho learn about superstitions in Scotland?

   _____

3. Which person is *not* superstitious?

   _____

4. Which of the following topics do the blog posters write about? Circle the letters of the correct answers.

   a. black cats   **c.** ladders   **e.** tests
   b. mirrors   **d.** New Year's   **f.** gifts

Read

A. Read the posts on Dan Jackson's blog. Time yourself. Write your start and end times and your total reading time. Then calculate your reading speed (words per minute) and write it in the progress chart on page 205.

Start time: _____   **End time:** _____   **Total time:** _____ (in seconds)

Reading speed:
566 words ÷ _____ (total time in seconds) x 60 = _____ words per minute

Adventures in English with Dan Jackson

Posted by Sungho from Seoul, South Korea

1 I'm Sungho from South Korea. Here are two superstitions from my culture and another one that I learned when I was studying

5 English in Scotland a few years ago. I hope you can use them in your book!

On the day of an important test, never wash your hair. If you do, Koreans say that your memories will be washed away with the

10 water. The result? You will forget everything you studied.

Here's another one from Korea: Never give a boyfriend or a girlfriend a pair of shoes. If you do, he or she will walk away from you and

15 leave you all alone.

I learned this one when I spent New Year's Eve in Scotland. I've always thought it was interesting. The Scots say that starting at midnight on December 31, it is bad luck to

20 leave your house before someone has visited you. That person is called a "first footer." First footers should bring a gift. If they don't, it can be bad luck. The best "first footers" are tall, black-haired men. They bring good luck for

25 the next twelve months. First footers who are female or who have red hair bring bad luck, even if they bring nice gifts! (I don't know about you, but I think if a nice red-haired girl came to my door with a gift, I might risk a little bad luck!)

30 Good luck with your project! I'm sure it's going to be successful.

Posted by Elena from Siberia

Great project idea! I'm not at all superstitious, but I think superstitions are

35 very interesting. And I like the idea of giving money to build cultural communication

and understanding. As I'm sure you know, Russia has a long history and lots and lots of superstitions. Here are just a few. If you like

40 them and want more, just let me know. BTW, I love your blog!

In Russia, we say that a stranger should not look at a newborn baby before it is a certain age (between two months and one year). And

45 when you do look at a baby, you should try not to say anything very nice. It will bring bad luck. Instead, you might say something like "Oh, what an ugly child!"

I believe that many cultures have

50 superstitions about mirrors, but I think the Russian ones are especially interesting. As in many other countries, Russians think it is very bad luck to break a mirror. But we also believe that you should never look in a

55 broken mirror. That is the very worst luck!

We also have rules about eating and drinking and looking in mirrors—never do them at the same time. If you eat and look in a mirror (even if it's not broken) at the same time,

60 you will "eat" all of your luck. The same is true for drinking; if you drink when you look in a mirror, you will "drink" your luck. So be careful with mirrors!

But mirrors can also have the opposite effect

65 in certain situations. For example, one of our superstitions says that if you forget something at home and have to go back for it, you will have bad luck. However, if you look in a mirror before you leave the house again, your

70 luck will change from bad to good.

Hope these were helpful! Good luck with your project.

B. Read the blog posts again, a little faster this time. Write your start and end times and your total reading time. Then calculate your reading speed (words per minute) and write it in the progress chart on page 205.

Start time: _____   End time: _____   Total time: _____ (in seconds)

Reading speed:
566 words ÷ _____ (total time in seconds) x 60 = _____ words per minute

C. Check your answers to the Before You Read questions on page 141. Are they correct? If not, correct them.

Comprehension Check

A. Complete the sentences with information from the blog.

Russia

In Russia it is bad luck to (1)_____.

It is also bad luck to (2)_____.

It is also bad luck to (3) _____,

but you can change your luck if you (4) _____.

South Korea

In South Korea, if you have an important test, (5) _____ because if

you do, (6) _____.

And never (7) _____ because if you do, (8) _____

_____.

Scotland

A "first footer" is (9) _____.

On New Year's Day, it is bad luck to (10) _____.

The first footers who bring the most luck are (11) _____, and they bring

gifts. First footers who bring the worst luck are (12) _____.

B. Check your answers for the comprehension questions in the Answer Key on page 206. Then calculate your score and write it in the progress chart on page 205.

_____ (my number correct) ÷ 12 x 100 = _____%

> THINK BEFORE YOU READ

A. Work with a partner. Look at the picture. Ask and answer the questions. If you don't know a word in English, ask your partner or look in your dictionary. Then write your new words on page 192.

    1. What is unusual about the people in the picture?

    2. At what kind of event do you think the picture was taken?

B. Work with a partner. Ask and answer the questions.

    1. Do you have any friends or family who are twins? If so, do the twins have a close relationship?

    2. What are some advantages of being a twin?

    3. What are some disadvantages of being a twin?

    4. Would you like to be a twin? Why or why not?

Two in One

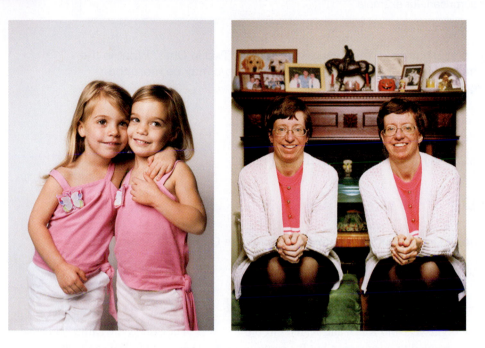

> PREPARE TO READ

A. Look at the words (and phrases) in the list. Write the number(s) next to each word to show what you know. You may be able to write more than one number next to some of the words. You will study all of these words in this chapter.

1. I can use the word in a sentence.

2. I know <u>one meaning</u> of the word.

3. I know <u>more than one meaning</u> of the word.

4. I know how to pronounce the word.

B. Work with a partner. Look at the pictures. Ask and answer the questions. If you don't know a word in English, ask your partner or look in your dictionary. Then write your new words on page 192.

1. Can you see any differences between the two little girls in the pictures? Can you see any differences between the two women?

2. Why do you think some twins continue to dress the same after they grow up?

3. Do you look like anyone in your family? Who?

_____ apart

_____ company

_____ except

_____ identical

_____ lie down

_____ matching

_____ separate

_____ shake

_____ style

_____ unless

Reading Skill: Understanding Tone

The *tone* of a reading shows you how the writer feels about the topic. To understand the writer's tone, pay attention to the way the details and the descriptions of people and events make you feel—happy, sad, angry, serious, excited, or surprised, for example.

C. Read the first ten lines of the newspaper article "Two in One." What is the tone of the reading? Check (✓) the answer(s). There may be more than one correct answer.

_____ **1.** angry   _____ **4.** sad

_____ **2.** excited   _____ **5.** serious

_____ **3.** funny   _____ **6.** surprised

> READ

Read "Two in One." Was your answer for Exercise C correct?

Two in One

1   Thirty-eight-year-old Karol and Karen Groom have never wanted to be anything but the same. They are **identical** twins, and they love it. In fact, they share everything—even an identity.

5   Karol: "We are the same, aren't we?"
Karen: "Yes, we're the same."
I ask if there are any differences. Two heads **shake** no.
Karen: "I can't think of any."
10   "So are you one person?" I ask.
Karen: "Think so."
Karol: "Yes, think so."
They always have their hair cut on the same day, in the same **style**. They always wear
15   exactly the same clothes.
Karol: "We always decide . . ."
Karen: " . . . the night before . . ."
Karol: " . . . what we're going to wear."

They dress the same "because we like it!"
20   They went to the same college, where they both studied business. When I ask questions, they look at each other.
Karen: "When did I leave my first job?"
Karol: "It's so long ago now . . ."
25   Karen: "I can't remember."
They both passed their driving test on the same day.
Karol: "But she passed in the morning."
Karen: "I passed in the morning . . ."
30   Karol: " . . . and I did it in the afternoon."
In 1993, aged twenty-seven, they left home—together. They now share a small house in a London suburb.[1] Their sitting room[2] is full of photographs of two little girls dressed
35   exactly the same: in **matching** red tops and kilts;[3] in red furry slippers[4] under the Christmas tree.[5] In these photos, even they don't know

---

[1] **suburb:** an area away from the center of a city, where a lot of people live

[2] **sitting room:** the main room in a house where people sit, watch TV, etc.

[3] **kilt:** a type of wool skirt with a pattern of lines and squares on it

[4] **slipper:** a soft shoe you wear inside your house

[5] **Christmas tree:** a tree that people put inside their house and decorate for Christmas

who is who. "We are cute, we are cute," says Karen, looking at the pictures. They love themselves very much, as they love each other, which is almost the same thing.

Upstairs, they share one small bedroom. They **lie down** there at exactly the same time and wake up together. They have never gone out alone to a movie, restaurant, or shopping. The only time they spend **apart** is during the day at their **separate** workplace desks. Karol calls Karen every morning to let her know she's arrived at work.

They are always laughing and smiling, enjoying each other's **company**. Do they even know what loneliness is?

Karol and Karen, together: "No!"

Karol and Karen are probably the happiest people I have ever met.

"You've always got company," says Karol. "Got company," says Karen.

But there must be disadvantages, right?

Karen: "I don't think there are any."

Karol: "**Except** we're not going to get married . . ."

Karen: " . . . **unless** twin boys come along. But we're not going to meet any. We're happy being single."

Karol: "Because then you only have to worry about . . ."

Karen: " . . . each other."

Karol: "We're happy as we are. We don't really . . ."

Karen: " . . . need to get married."

Karol: "We're happy and close as we are."

Vocabulary Check

Circle the letter of the correct answer to complete each sentence. The boldfaced words are the target words.

1. We will go to the beach **unless** it's _____.

    a. summer   **b.** sunny   **c.** cold

2. I would have dinner with you, **except** I _____.

    a. already ate   **b.** am hungry   **c.** like the food

3. I'm going to **lie down**. I am _____.

    a. hungry   **b.** late   **c.** sick

4. They have **separate** lives. They don't spend much time with _____.

    a. each other   **b.** other people   **c.** their children

5. When you have **company**, you _____.

    a. own a business   **b.** make money   **c.** are not alone

6. That _____ isn't my **style**.

    a. dress   **b.** food   **c.** homework

(continued on next page)

7. When they were **apart**, they _____.

    a. called each other every day   **b.** lived in the same house   **c.** spent time together

8. These shoes don't **match**. They are _____.

    a. the same size   **b.** the wrong color   **c.** too big

9. Those two trees are _____, but they are not **identical**.

    a. different   **b.** similar   **c.** the same

10. I **shake** when I am very cold. My body _____ in order to get warm.

    a. moves   **b.** sleeps   **c.** hurts

> READ

Read "Two in One" again and complete the comprehension exercises. As you work, keep the reading goal in mind.

> 📖 **READING GOAL:** To learn about two sisters with a special relationship

Comprehension Check

A. Which sentence <u>best</u> describes Karen and Karol Groom? Check (✓) the answer.

_____ **1.** They're curious. They ask a lot of questions.

_____ **2.** They're close. They finish each other's sentences.

_____ **3.** They are lonely. They wish they were married.

B. Read the statements about Karol and Karen. Write *T* (true) or *F* (false). If it is not possible to tell, write *?*.

_____ **1.** They can identify each other in their childhood photographs.

_____ **2.** They dress the same.

_____ **3.** They are never apart.

_____ **4.** They work in the same office.

_____ **5.** They have similar jobs.

_____ **6.** They have separate bedrooms.

_____ **7.** They will get married to twin brothers.

_____ **8.** They feel like one person.

C. What do Karol and Karen share? Take notes in the chart. Include as much information as you can. Try not to look back at the reading.

Physical appearance (the way they look)	*same hairstyle,*
Daily activities (what they do every day)	*go to bed at the same time,*
Their past	*studied business,*
Their future	*live together,*
Their feelings about each other	*love each other very much,*

D. Work with a partner. Compare the information in your charts. Then discuss what surprised you the most about Karol and Karen Groom.

> ## DISCUSS

Work in small groups. Ask and answer the questions.

1. Are Karol and Karen lucky to have such a close relationship? Why or why not?

2. Should the parents of twins help them to become independent of each other? For example, should they dress them in different clothes? Put them in separate classes in school? Why or why not?

Identical Strangers

> PREPARE TO READ

A. Look at the words (and phrases) in the list. Write the number(s) next to each word to show what you know. You may be able to write more than one number next to some of the words. You will study all of these words in this chapter.

1. I can use the word in a sentence.

2. I know <u>one meaning</u> of the word.

3. I know <u>more than one meaning</u> of the word.

4. I know how to pronounce the word.

B. Work with a partner. Look at the picture. Ask and answer the question. If you don't know a word in English, ask your partner or look in your dictionary. Then write your new words on page 192.

What is the relationship between the women in the picture?

C. Preview the magazine article "Identical Strangers" on the next page. What is the tone of the reading? Check (✓) the answer(s).

_____ **1.** angry	_____ **3.** funny	_____ **5.** serious
_____ **2.** excited	_____ **4.** sad	_____ **6.** surprised

_____ agency

_____ in case

_____ inspect

_____ knee

_____ legal

_____ publish

_____ result

_____ run into

_____ shocked

_____ the news

READ

Read "Identical Strangers." Were your answers for Exercises B and C correct?

Identical Strangers

1   Elyse Schein and Paula Bernstein were adopted when they were babies. They grew up in different families. They knew that they were adopted. But they didn't know each other. They
5   were thirty-five years old when Elyse found out from an Internet search that she had an identical twin.

Paula remembers the day when she got **the news**. "It was a spring afternoon . . . I walk in
10   the door and the phone is ringing . . . And a woman [from an adoption **agency**] on the other end of the line confirmed[1] that I was in fact Paula Bernstein and I was adopted. And then she said, 'Well, I've got some news for you. I thought
15   I should tell you **in case** you were walking down Fifth Avenue[2] and **ran into** someone who looks exactly like you.' And then she said, '. . . You've got a twin who's looking for you.'"

Paula was **shocked**. "You know, I thought I
20   knew who I was, and suddenly my identity was . . . changed . . . "

Two days later, the sisters met at a café in New York City. Paula talks about that first meeting. "That was like, you know, monkeys in
25   a zoo[3] . . . we were . . . **inspecting** each other's bodies . . . And I remember I said, 'Do you have chubby[4] **knees**?' And I . . . saw that her knees were quite cute. And I always thought of mine as kind of chubby. So I thought, but why
30   did she get the cute knees?"

But Paula had another, more important question. Why were they separated? Why did they grow up without each other? The answer is shocking. When they were born, the
35   adoption agency entered them in a research study.[5] Because of the study, they were separated when they were only a few months old. What was the purpose of the study? The researchers wanted to find out which is
40   more important to human identity, genes[6] or environment.[7]

The people who adopted them did not have the chance to adopt both little girls. Why not? They did not know the truth: that the child
45   they were adopting had an identical twin. Today, this kind of research is not **legal**. But at the time, it was.

What were the **results** of the study? No one knows. The study was finished, but it was never
50   **published**. And no one can read it, either. The researcher,[8] Dr. Peter Neubauer, gave the study to Yale University, but with one condition: No one can look at it until 2066. If they can hold on until then, Paula and Elyse will be ninety-
55   eight years old.

---

[1] **confirm:** say or prove that something is true

[2] **Fifth Avenue:** a main street in New York City and one of the major shopping streets in the world

[3] **zoo:** a place where many different animals are kept so that people can see them

[4] **chubby:** slightly fat

[5] **research study:** serious work done to find out more about a particular subject

[6] **gene:** a part of a cell in a living thing that controls how it develops

[7] **environment:** the situations, things, people, etc., that affect the way in which people live and work

[8] **researcher:** someone who studies a subject in detail

Vocabulary Check

Complete the sentences with the boldfaced words from the reading.

1. I work at a travel _____. I help people plan their vacations.

2. You should wear a raincoat _____ it rains.

3. She _____ her first book when she was only eighteen.

4. Last week I _____ an old friend from college. I was really surprised to see her.

5. Why are the police _____ his car? Did he do something wrong?

6. You can't drive without a license. It is not _____.

7. I took my exams last week, but I don't know if I passed. I am waiting for the _____.

8. Did you hear _____? My son is getting married!

9. This skirt is too short. It doesn't cover my _____. Can you make it a little longer?

10. Everyone was _____ when he walked in the door. We thought he was in another country!

> READ AGAIN

Read "Identical Strangers" again and complete the comprehension exercises on the next page. As you work, keep the reading goal in mind.

> READING GOAL: To understand what happened to Elyse Schein and Paula Bernstein

Comprehension Check

A. Read the statements about the reading. Write *T* (true) or *F* (false). If it is not possible to tell, write *?*.

_____ 1. Elyse found out that she had a twin before Paula did.

_____ 2. Elyse was looking for Paula on Fifth Avenue.

_____ 3. Paula's adoptive parents didn't want to adopt Elyse.

_____ 4. Elyse's adoptive parents didn't know about Paula.

_____ 5. Elyse and Paula grew up apart.

_____ 6. Paula is happy that she has a twin sister.

_____ 7. The girls' mother entered them in a scientific study.

_____ 8. Dr. Neubauer wanted to know whether genes or environment is more important.

_____ 9. Dr. Neubauer's study was legal.

_____ 10. You can find the results of Dr. Neubauer's study on the Internet.

_____ 11. Paula and Elyse would like to read the results of the study.

B. Put the events from the story in the correct order. Write *1* for the first thing that happened, *2* for the second thing, and so on. Try not to look back at the reading.

_____ The adoption agency entered Paula and Elyse in a scientific study on identical twins.

_____ Paula and Elyse found out about Dr. Neubauer's study.

_____ Paula and Elyse might be able to read Dr. Neubauer's study.

____*1*___ Paula and Elyse's mother gave the girls to an adoption agency.

_____ Paula and Elyse were adopted by different families.

_____ Paula and Elyse grew up without knowing that they were twins.

_____ Paula and Elyse met when they were thirty-five years old.

_____ As a part of the study, Paula and Elyse were separated.

C. Work with a partner. Check your answers for Exercises A and B. Look back at the reading and correct any mistakes.

⟩ DISCUSS

Work in small groups. Ask and answer the questions.

1. Today it is not legal to do the kind of study that Dr. Neubauer did. Why not? What is the problem with that kind of study?

2. Why do you think Dr. Neubauer never published the results of his study? Why didn't he want anyone to read the results until 2066?

⟩ VOCABULARY SKILL BUILDING

Vocabulary Skill: Phrasal Verbs

A *phrasal verb* is a verb that is followed by one or two small words, called *particles*. A phrasal verb has a special meaning. That meaning is different from the meaning of the verb by itself.

EXAMPLE:

Alice **ran into** Betty yesterday on Fifth Avenue.

Run into is a phrasal verb. The particle is the preposition *into*. The meaning of *run into* is different from the meaning of *run*. *Run into* means to meet someone by chance.

Sometimes you can guess the meaning of a phrasal verb from the context. Other times you will need to look in your dictionary. In most dictionaries, the definitions of phrasal verbs come at the end of the verb entry.

A. Read the sentences. Underline the phrasal verbs. The phrasal verbs are target words from the readings in this book.

1. It really is a small world. When I was in Paris, I ran into an old classmate.

2. She lost her job when her boss found out that she was stealing money.

3. We can't hold on much longer. Unless business gets better very soon, we will need to sell the store.

4. He ran away when he was fifteen years old. His parents never found him.

B. Write the letter of the correct definition next to the phrasal verb.

_____ **1.** run into	**a.** to continue to do something difficult until it gets better
_____ **2.** find out	**b.** to leave a place in order to escape from someone or something
_____ **3.** hold on	**c.** to meet someone by chance
_____ **4.** run away	**d.** to learn information after trying to discover it or by chance

Learn the Vocabulary

Strategy

Using the Keyword Technique

There are many ways to remember the meaning of a new word. The keyword technique works well for many learners. Here's how it works:

1. Look at the new word, and choose a *keyword*. A keyword is a word in your native language that sounds similar to the beginning or all of the new word in English. Look at the example from a native speaker of Spanish.

EXAMPLE:

New word = *knee*

Keyword (Spanish word that sounds similar) = *niño (boy)*

2. Imagine a picture where the meaning of the new word and the meaning of the keyword are connected in some way. The connection can be strange. In fact, strange pictures are often easier to remember!

3. To remember the word *knee* in English, think of the image of the *niño* on the woman's knee.

EXAMPLE:

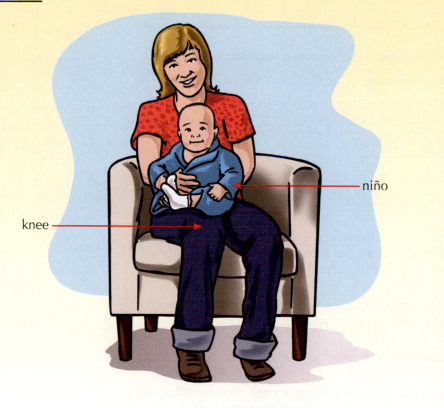

knee

niño

(continued on next page)

4. If you like to draw, you can draw the picture on the back side of your word card, with the English word on the front side.

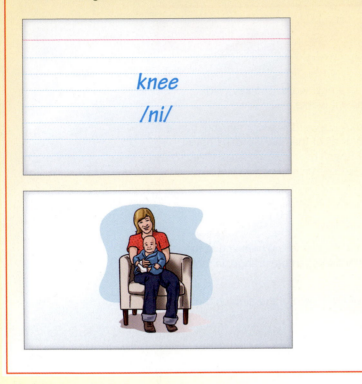

knee
/ni/

A. Write five target words from the unit. Then write a keyword for each.

Target word   **Keyword**

1. _____ = _____

2. _____ = _____

3. _____ = _____

4. _____ = _____

5. _____ = _____

B. Now imagine a picture to connect the new word and the keyword for each of the new words in Exercise A. Draw the picture on one side of a word card. Write the new word on the other side of the card.

C. Show your cards to a classmate. Explain your pictures by pronouncing the keywords and telling the meanings in your native language.

D. Add the cards to your other cards. Review all of your cards with a partner.

E. Go back to the vocabulary list at the beginning of each chapter. What did you learn about the target words? Add your numbers to the lists.

Vocabulary Practice 10, see page 202

> THINK BEFORE YOU READ

A. Work with a partner. Look at the pictures. Check (✓) the things you see. Keep looking until you see all six of the images. If you don't know a word in English, ask your partner or look in your dictionary. Then write your new words on page 192.

_____ **1.** a duck   _____ **4.** a young woman

_____ **2.** a goblet   _____ **5.** an old woman

_____ **3.** a rabbit   _____ **6.** two faces

B. Which of the things are easy for you to remember? Which are difficult? Write _E_ (easy) or _D_ (difficult). Share your answers with a partner.

_____ **1.** people's faces

_____ **2.** people's names

_____ **3.** happy times from your childhood

_____ **4.** unhappy times from your childhood

C. Work with a partner. Ask and answer the questions.

1. Have you heard the expression "Seeing is believing"?

2. What do you think it means?

Hugging Bugs Bunny

> PREPARE TO READ

A. Look at the words (and phrases) in the list. Write the number(s) next to each word to show what you know. You may be able to write more than one number next to some of the words. You will study all of these words in this chapter.

1. I can use the word in a sentence.

2. I know <u>one meaning</u> of the word.

3. I know <u>more than one meaning</u> of the word.

4. I know how to pronounce the word.

B. Work with a partner. Look at the pictures. Ask and answer the questions. If you don't know a word in English, ask your partner or look in your dictionary. Then write your new words on page 192.

1. Who are the characters in the pictures?

2. Where was the third picture taken? Have you ever visited a place like that? If not, would you like to?

_____ accuse

_____ childhood

_____ create

_____ go free

_____ guilty

_____ memory

_____ purpose

_____ sight

_____ touch

_____ victim

Reading Skill: Recognizing Text References

Writers often *refer to* an idea from a previous sentence or paragraph in a reading. It is important to understand which idea the writer is referring to.

Look at the examples from "Hugging Bugs Bunny."

EXAMPLES:

Can we trust our memories? Psychologist Elizabeth Loftus doesn't think so.

= that we can trust our memories

They really believe their memories. And that is why it can be difficult to know if a memory is real.

= that they really believe their memories

C. Preview the newspaper science article "Hugging Bugs Bunny" on the next page. Then answer the questions.

1. Can we trust our memories?

2. What is a false memory?

3. Why do the police need to be careful about how they ask questions?

Read "Hugging Bugs Bunny." Check your answers for Exercise C on page 159.

Hugging Bugs Bunny

1 Can we trust our **memories**? Psychologist[1] Elizabeth Loftus doesn't think so. Loftus is an expert on false memories. A false memory is a memory of something that never happened. Are
5 people with false memories lying? Not at all, says Loftus. They really believe their memories. And that is why it can be difficult to know if a memory is real.

In one experiment on false memories,
10 Loftus talked to people about their **childhoods**. They didn't know each other, but 36 percent of them had the same memory. What was it? They remembered hugging Bugs Bunny at Disneyland. But wait a minute. Bugs Bunny
15 is not a Disney character, and he was never at Disneyland. The people's memories were false.

How could a group of strangers all have the same false memory? Loftus says it is easy to put a false memory into someone's mind.
20 How? You just talk to the person. In the Bugs Bunny experiment, Loftus talked to people who had visited Disneyland as children. Then she asked them about Bugs Bunny. She asked if he had soft ears. She asked if his body was furry.[2]
25 Later, more than one-third falsely remembered hugging Bugs Bunny.

When we remember something, we use all of our senses: **sight**, **touch**, taste, smell, and hearing. That is why Loftus used the words
30 "furry" and "soft" in the experiment. Those words helped people imagine the experience. They saw Bugs Bunny in their imagination. They felt his soft fur. It seemed so real. They were sure it really happened.

35 But what is the **purpose** of the Bugs Bunny experiment? Loftus says it shows the dangers of false memory. Of course, a false memory of Bugs Bunny is not dangerous, but imagine this situation. A man hits a woman on the head.
40 Then he steals her car. The police ask the **victim** if the thief smelled of cigarettes. In fact, he did not, but after the woman hears the question, she becomes 100 percent sure that he did. She adds the smell of cigarettes to her real memory and
45 **creates** a false memory. The police then **accuse** the wrong person, a smoker. As a result, they never find the **guilty** man. He's a nonsmoker, so the police don't even look for him.

That is why the police need to be very
50 careful about how they ask questions, says Loftus. If they aren't careful, they won't find the truth. Instead, they will find only false memories, and the real criminals will **go free**.

---

[1] **psychologist:** someone who studies the mind
[2] **furry:** covered with thick, soft hair

Vocabulary Check

Write T (true) or F (false) for each statement. Then correct the false statements to make them true. The boldfaced words are the target words.

_____ 1. The **victim** of a crime is the criminal.

_____ 2. When you **create** something, you make something old.

_____ 3. If the police **accuse** you of a crime, you should call a lawyer.

_____ 4. The **purpose** of an umbrella is to protect you from the rain.

_____ 5. **Childhood** is the time in your life when you are young.

_____ 6. Our sense of **touch** makes it possible for us to feel things with our bodies.

_____ 7. We use our sense of **sight** when we listen to music.

_____ 8. When a criminal **goes free**, he or she goes to prison.

_____ 9. People who are **guilty** of crimes did nothing wrong.

_____ 10. **Memories** are formed in our brains.

> READ AGAIN

Read "Hugging Bugs Bunny" again and complete the comprehension exercises. As you work, keep the reading goal in mind.

> 📖 **READING GOAL:** To explain how a false memory is formed

Comprehension Check

A. Check (✓) the main idea of "Hugging Bugs Bunny."

_____ 1. Many of our childhood memories are probably false memories.

_____ 2. It is easy to create a false memory and make someone believe it is real.

_____ 3. The police often create false memories when they ask crime victims questions.

B. Find the sentences in the reading. What do the underlined words refer to? Circle the letter of the correct answer. The numbers in parentheses are the paragraphs where you can find the sentences.

1. Later, <u>more than one-third</u> falsely remembered hugging Bugs Bunny. (3)

   More than one-third refers to _____.

   a. the children at Disneyland

   b. the people in Loftus's experiment

2. <u>That</u> is why Loftus used the words "furry" and "soft" in the experiment. (4)

   That refers to _____.

   a. that we remember something

   b. that we use all of our senses to remember things

3. They were sure <u>it</u> really happened. (4)

   It refers to _____.

   a. the experience of hugging Bugs Bunny

   b. their imagination

4. Of course, a false memory of Bugs Bunny is not dangerous, but imagine <u>this situation</u>. (5)

   This situation refers to _____.

   a. Loftus's experiment

   b. a man hits a woman over the head

5. In fact, he did not, but after the woman hears <u>the question</u>, she becomes 100 percent sure that he did. (5)

   The question refers to _____.

   a. Did the thief hit the woman?

   b. Did the thief smell of cigarettes?

6. <u>That</u> is why the police need to be very careful about how they ask questions, says Loftus. (6)

   That refers to _____.

   a. that they might accuse the wrong person of a crime

   b. the experiment that Loftus did

C. Put the pictures in order to show how a false memory is formed. Write *1* next to the first thing that happened, *2* next to the second, and so on. Try not to look back at the reading.

_____

_____   _____

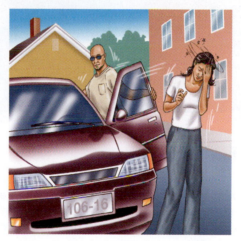

_____

> DISCUSS

Work in small groups. Describe a powerful memory from your childhood. If you have a photograph that is connected to the memory, bring it in to show your classmates. Use the following questions to help you.

Who is in the memory?   When did it happen?
What happened?   How did you feel?
Where did it happen?   Why do you think you remembered it?

> PREPARE TO READ

A. Look at the words in the list. Write the number(s) next to each word to show what you know. You may be able to write more than one number next to some of the words. You will study all of these words in this chapter.

1. I can use the word in a sentence.

2. I know <u>one meaning</u> of the word.

3. I know <u>more than one meaning</u> of the word.

4. I know how to pronounce the word.

B. Work with a partner. Look at the picture. Ask and answer the questions. If you don't know a word in English, ask your partner or look in your dictionary. Then write your new words on page 192.

1. Who are the people in the picture? What are they doing?

2. Do you like shows like the one in the picture? Why or why not?

3. What do you think of when you hear the word "magic"?

_____ bright

_____ clap

_____ hide

_____ illusion

_____ image

_____ magician

_____ remain

_____ secret

_____ tight

_____ visual

Reading Skill: Making Inferences

Sometimes the writer does not say everything directly in the text. Instead, the reader has to think about the information in the text and make his or her own conclusion based on that information. That conclusion is called an *inference*. An inference is stronger than a guess. A guess might be correct or incorrect. An inference is probably correct because it is based on real information in the text.

EXAMPLE:

Yesterday John was coughing a lot, and today he's not in class.

Inference: John is sick.

C. Read the first paragraph of "Is Seeing Really Believing?," an essay from a book on magic, on the next page. Then check (✓) the inference(s) that you can make based on the information in that paragraph.

_____ **1.** A magician is practicing before a show.

_____ **2.** A magician is doing a magic show in front of a lot of people.

_____ **3.** The beautiful woman is the magician's wife.

_____ **4.** The beautiful woman works with the magician.

> READ

Read "Is Seeing Really Believing?" Were your inferences for Exercise C on page 165 correct?

∽ Is Seeing Really Believing? ∝

1   All eyes are on the beautiful woman wearing the very white, very **tight** dress. The **magician** tells us to watch carefully. He says that he will change the color of her dress from white to red. He **claps** his hands, and the lights dim[1] for less than a second. Then we see the woman again. She is standing under a **bright** red light.

5   The magician stands next to her. He is smiling at his little joke. We all laugh. Everyone agrees that he did turn her dress red—along with the rest of her body. Then the magician asks everyone to look at the woman again. He claps his hands, and the red lights go dark. Less than a second later, the white houselights[2] come on. The woman's dress is red! The Great Tomsoni has fooled us again!

10   But what is The Great Tomsoni's **secret**? Does he have magical powers? No, he has something much more powerful. He understands how the human brain works. He knows that when the red lights go dark, the red **image** of the woman **remains** in our brains for about 100 milliseconds.[3] That red *afterimage* covers the real woman in front of us. In those 100 milliseconds, the woman removes her white

15   dress. Under it she is wearing a copy of the white dress—except, of course, it is red.

Magicians like The Great Tomsoni are experts in human psychology.[4] Their "magic" is the result of careful training. Over hundreds of years of practice, magicians have learned how to create many different kinds of **illusions**. In the red dress trick, The Great Tomsoni uses a **visual** illusion, an afterimage, to **hide** the trick.

20   Magicians also use cognitive[5] illusions. Like visual illusions, cognitive illusions change the way we see reality. But cognitive illusions do not fool our senses. Instead, they play with the way that we think. For example, in the red dress trick, The Great Tomsoni uses a simple cognitive illusion. The woman's dress looks tight. The magician knows that when most people see the tight dress, they will

25   never imagine that there is another dress under it. But of course there is.

Then The Great Tomsoni uses another cognitive illusion. He makes us believe that his joke with the red light *is* the trick. We think that he has already finished the trick, so we relax. We aren't watching as carefully as before. Of course, that was his real purpose. This is the perfect moment for the real trick. When we

30   see the woman in the red dress, we will believe that there is only one possible explanation. For that one moment, we will all believe in magic.

---

[1] **dim:** become less bright

[2] **houselights:** the lights in a theater

[3] **millisecond:** one thousandth of a second

[4] **psychology:** the study of the mind and how it works

[5] **cognitive:** relating to the process of understanding and learning something

Vocabulary Check

Complete the sentences with the boldfaced words from the reading.

1. I wear my sunglasses when the sun is very _____.

2. Our teacher _____ his hands when he wants to get our attention.

3. Shy children sometimes _____ behind their parents.

4. The _____ can do a lot of tricks. Some people think he has magical powers.

5. My stomach hurts because my pants are too _____.

6. A small room will look bigger if you hang a lot of mirrors. Designers create _____ like this all of the time.

7. He has a(n) _____ of how he will look in twenty years.

8. If my wife _____ in London, I will stay, too.

9. I can't tell you what she told me because it's a _____.

10. Painters create _____ images of their ideas.

> READ AGAIN

Read "Is Seeing Really Believing?" again and complete the comprehension exercises on the next page. As you work, keep the reading goal in mind.

READING GOAL: To understand how the red dress trick works

Comprehension Check

A. Find the sentences in the reading. What do the underlined words mean or refer to? Circle the letter of the correct answer. The numbers in parentheses are the paragraphs where you can find the sentences.

1. But what is <u>The Great Tomsoni's secret</u>? (3)

   The Great Tomsoni's secret refers to _____.

   a. his powerful magic

   b. his understanding of the human brain

2. Instead, <u>they</u> play with the way that we think. (5)

   They refers to _____.

   a. cognitive illusions

   b. our senses

3. The magician knows that when most people see the tight dress, they will never imagine that there is another dress under <u>it</u>. (5)

   It refers to _____.

   a. the tight dress

   b. the red dress

4. Of course, <u>that</u> was his real purpose. (6)

   That means _____.

   a. that we aren't watching carefully

   b. that he has already finished the trick

5. <u>This</u> is the perfect moment for the real trick. (6)

   This refers to _____.

   a. when we aren't watching carefully

   b. his real purpose

6. When we see the woman in the red dress, we will believe that there is only <u>one possible explanation</u>. (6)

   One possible explanation means _____.

   a. magic

   b. one moment

B. Put the pictures in order to show how the red dress trick works. Write *1* next to the first thing that happened, *2* next to the second, and so on. Try not to look back at the reading.

 _____

 _____

 _____

 _____

 _____

 _____

> DISCUSS

Work in small groups. Ask and answer the questions.

1. Is magic popular in your culture? Explain your answer.

2. What magical powers would you like to have?

3. Do you know how to do a magic trick? If so, show the class. Can the class guess how you did it?

> VOCABULARY SKILL BUILDING

Vocabulary Skill: Roots and Prefixes

Some words in English are built from a *root* (a Latin or Greek word part) plus a prefix or suffix, or *both* a prefix and suffix. Like a prefix, the root has a special meaning, but it is not a word by itself. Instead, it appears as a part of other words in the same word family. For example, *-vis-* is a root. It means *see*. The target word *visual* contains the root *-vis-* and an adjective suffix, *-al*.

If you know the meaning of common roots and prefixes in English, it will help you guess the meaning of other words that contain them.

Look at the chart of common roots and prefixes. The example words were target words in previous chapters. Complete the chart with the correct meanings from the list. Your understanding of the meanings of the target words will help you guess the meanings of the roots and prefixes.

across	inside	look at	say/speak
before	lead	remember	~~see~~
between/among	live	same	together/with

Root	Example	Meaning of root
-vis-	visual	*see*
-dict-	predict	
-viv-	survive	
-spect-	inspect	
-duc-	introduction	
-mem-, -memor-	memory	

Prefix	Example	Meaning of prefix
tran-, trans-	translate	
co-, con-,	connect	
identi-	identity, identify, identical	
inter-	interpreter	
pre-	predict	
intro-	introduction	

Learn the Vocabulary

Using Word Parts to Guess Meaning

In Unit 9, you practiced using prefixes to help you guess the meaning of new words. You can use word roots in the same way.

EXAMPLE:

*You can **pre**dict the weather a day in advance but not a month in advance.*

Word Part Meaning:

***pre*- = before   *-dict-* = say/speak**

Context:

What can you predict?	the weather
When can you predict it?	a day in advance
When can't you predict it?	a month in advance

Definition:

When you **predict** something, you *say* what will happen in the future, *before* it happens.

A. Write a definition for each boldfaced word. Use the word part strategy and the context.

1. We could find her in the crowd because she was wearing a **vivid** red dress.

   Definition of **vivid**: _____

2. A lot of famous people write and publish their **memoirs** before they die.

   Definition of **memoir**: _____

3. I love soccer, but I don't like to play. I prefer to be a **spectator**.

   Definition of **spectator**: _____

4. When you travel from Boston to Europe, you make a **transatlantic** trip.

   Definition of **transatlantic**: _____

B. Now find the words from Exercise A in your dictionary and check your definitions.

C. Go back to the vocabulary list at the beginning of each chapter. What did you learn about the target words? Add your numbers to the lists.

Vocabulary Practice 11, see page 203

> THINK BEFORE YOU READ

A. Work with a partner. Look at the picture. Ask and answer the questions. If you don't know a word in English, ask your partner or look in your dictionary. Then write your new words on page 192.

  1. What is happening? What is the name of the movie in the picture?

  2. Look up the words *madness* and *collective* in a dictionary. Who in the picture is mad? What do you think *collective madness* means?

B. Work in pairs or small groups. Read the two stories. Which one is an example of collective madness? Check (✓) it. Then explain your answer.

  _____ **1.** People at a party eat fruit salad. They get sick. The police find out that someone put poison in the fruit salad.

  _____ **2.** One person at a party says that the food tastes strange. Then she gets sick. Soon almost everyone at the party is sick. The doctors can't find anything wrong with them or the food.

CHAPTER 23

Tulip Fever

▶ PREPARE TO READ

A. Look at the words (and phrases) in the list. Write the number(s) next to each word to show what you know. You may be able to write more than one number next to some of the words. You will study all of these words in this chapter.

1. I can use the word in a sentence.

2. I know <u>one meaning</u> of the word.

3. I know <u>more than one meaning</u> of the word.

4. I know how to pronounce the word.

B. Work with a partner. Look at the picture. Ask and answer the questions. If you don't know a word in English, ask your partner or look in your dictionary. Then write your new words on page 192.

1. What is the name of the flower in the picture? Does it grow in your country? Which country is famous for this flower?

2. Which flowers do you like? Do you have a favorite flower?

_____ borrow

_____ come to one's senses

_____ farmer

_____ fever

_____ gardener

_____ market

_____ ordinary

_____ trade

_____ wealthy

_____ worth

A *figurative* word or expression is used in a different way from the way it is usually used.

EXAMPLE:

Wild used with its usual meaning:

*A lion is a **wild** animal.* = A lion is an animal that lives in a natural state, <u>without being controlled</u> by humans.

Wild used figuratively:

*I am **wild** about lions!* = I love lions so much that <u>I lose control</u> of my emotions when I talk about them.

In this example, even if you already know the usual meaning of *wild*, you will need to use the context and a little imagination to understand the figurative meaning.

C. Preview the excerpt "Tulip Fever" on the next page. Then answer the questions.

1. The title of the reading is "Tulip Fever." What do you think the title means? (If you don't know what *fever* means, look in your dictionary.)

2. What is the main topic of "Tulip Fever"? Check (✓) it.

_____ **a.** an illness caused by tulips that killed many people

_____ **b.** an insect that killed almost all of the tulips in Holland

_____ **c.** a time when people sold everything they had in order to buy tulips

READ

Read "Tulip Fever." Were your answers for Exercise C correct?

ஒ Tulip Fever ஐ

1   Tulips—tall, beautiful, brightly colored flowers—have an interesting history. Today, you can see tulips all over Holland, a region of the Netherlands. Holland did not always have tulips, however. No one is sure where the first tulips came from, but we do know that they were once very popular with Turkish rulers.

5   In Turkey, the tulip was a flower for the rich and powerful. There were many laws to limit who could grow and sell tulips. The tulip was not a flower for the **ordinary** person.

   In the 1500s, Europeans heard about these special flowers, and they wanted some of their own. Tulip bulbs from Turkey were sent to the Royal Medicinal
10 Gardens in Prague.[1] The **gardener** there was named Clusius. Some years later, Clusius moved to Holland. He took the tulip bulbs with him. He then planted them at the Leiden Botanical Garden.[2]

   At that time, merchants[3] in Holland were getting very rich from **trading** with other countries. These **wealthy** Dutch merchants built large, expensive houses.
15 Like the Turkish rulers before them, they wanted tulips for their gardens. But there was a problem. Clusius did not want to share his tulips. To get them, people had to sneak into the botanical garden and steal the bulbs.

   Because tulips were so difficult to get and so many people wanted them, they became very expensive. At first only wealthy merchants could buy them. But in
20 1630 a new profession began: tulip trading. Traders bought tulip bulbs and resold them at a much higher price. It seemed an easy way to make money fast.

   Soon everyone was **borrowing** money for tulip bulbs. Ordinary **farmers** and workers risked everything to buy them. In 1633 one man traded his farmhouse for three bulbs. In 1636 one bulb sold for 5,200 guilders.[4] That was as much money
25 as a rich merchant made in a year! The whole country was wild for tulips. Soon, everyone had tulip **fever**.

   Today, we can see that the Dutch[5] were not thinking **clearly**. They believed that tulip prices would rise forever. But then the fever broke.[6] The traders **came to their senses** first. From one day to the next, they stopped buying tulip bulbs.
30 The tulip **markets** crashed. Bulbs **worth** 5,000 guilders one day were worth nothing the next. Ordinary people lost everything: their homes, their land, their farms, and their life savings.

   Tulip fever was a disaster for ordinary people in Holland, but the financial markets survived. Today, the tulip is no longer a flower just for the rich. That is
35 good news for the Dutch, who make hundreds of millions of dollars a year from tulip sales to ordinary people all over the world.

---

[1] **Prague:** a city in eastern Europe in what is now called the Czech Republic

[2] **botanical garden:** a large public garden with many types of flowers and plants

[3] **merchant:** someone who buys and sells large quantities of goods

[4] **guilder:** the money of the Netherlands

[5] **the Dutch:** the people of the Netherlands

[6] **break:** end

Vocabulary Check

Write *T* (true) or *F* (false) for each statement. Then correct the false statements to make them true. The boldfaced words are the target words.

_____ **1.** People with a **fever** are usually ill.

_____ **2.** **Gardeners** work inside.

_____ **3.** An **ordinary** person is strange.

_____ **4.** When you **come to your senses**, you realize that you did something clever.

_____ **5.** **Farmers** work with plants and animals.

_____ **6.** When you **borrow** money, you don't need to pay it back.

_____ **7.** You can buy and sell things in a **market**.

_____ **8.** **Trading** and selling are the same.

_____ **9.** If you own a house **worth** $20 million, you are probably **wealthy**.

> READ AGAIN

Read "Tulip Fever" again and complete the comprehension exercises. As you work, keep the reading goal in mind.

> 📖 **READING GOAL:** To understand how and why "tulip fever" happened

Comprehension Check

A. Look at the sentences from the reading. Write *U* next to the sentences in which the underlined words are used in their usual way. Write *F* next to the sentences that contain figurative language.

___*U*___ **1.** No one is sure where the first tulips came from, but we do know that they were once very popular with Turkish rulers.

___*F*___ **2.** The traders came to their senses first.

_____ **3.** At that time, merchants in Holland were getting very rich from trading with other countries.

_____ **4.** Soon, everyone had tulip fever.

_____ **5.** But then the fever broke.

_____ **6.** The tulip markets crashed.

_____ **7.** Tulip fever was a disaster for ordinary people in Holland, but the financial markets survived.

B. Answer the questions in your own words. Many of the answers are not in the reading. You will need to infer them.

1. Ordinary Turkish people could not grow or buy tulips. What do you think the reason was?

   _____

   _____

2. Why did wealthy Dutch merchants want tulips and not some other flower for their gardens?

   _____

   _____

3. Why didn't Clusius want to share his tulip bulbs?

   _____

   _____

4. Why did tulip bulbs become so expensive in Holland?

   _____

   _____

5. Why did ordinary people sell their land, houses, and animals to buy tulip bulbs?

   _____

   _____

6. Why did the tulip markets finally crash?

   _____

   _____

7. Who lost the most—the professional tulip traders, the Dutch merchants, or ordinary people? Who lost the least? Why?

   _____

   _____

C. Work with a partner. Compare and explain your answers for Exercise B. Correct any mistakes.

> DISCUSS

Work in small groups. Ask and answer the questions.

1. Do you buy flowers? If so, what kind? Why?

2. Can you think of something today that is as valuable as tulips were in the 1500s? Do you think it will always be so special? Why or why not?

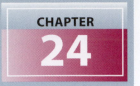
The Dancing Plague

Dancing villagers collapse
in exhaustion

> PREPARE TO READ

A. Look at the words in the list. Write the number(s) next to each word to show what you know. You may be able to write more than one number next to some of the words. You will study all of these words in this chapter.

   1. I can use the word in a sentence.

   2. I know <u>one meaning</u> of the word.

   3. I know <u>more than one meaning</u> of the word.

   4. I know how to pronounce the word.

B. Work with a partner. Look at the picture and the caption. Ask and answer the questions. If you don't know a word in English, ask your partner or look in your dictionary. Then write your new words on page 192.

   1. What do you think is happening in the picture?

   2. The title of the reading is "The Dancing Plague." What is a *plague*? How could dancing be a plague?

C. Preview the excerpt "The Dancing Plague" on the next page. Then on a separate sheet of paper, write three questions that you think the reading will answer.

_____ crop

_____ desperate

_____ dozen

_____ frightened

_____ historian

_____ spirit

_____ spread

_____ suffer

_____ terrible

 **READ**

Read "The Dancing Plague." Underline the answers to your questions for Exercise C.

∽ The Dancing Plague ∾

1   In July of 1518, a woman went out into a street in Strasbourg, France, and started to dance. By the end of the week, there were thirty-four more dancers. Within a month, there were 400. The people continued to dance and dance. They never stopped. As a result, many of them **suffered** heart attacks,[1] strokes,[2] and
5   exhaustion.[3] By the end of the summer, **dozens** in the city were dead.

Historian John Waller wrote a book about that terrible July in Strasbourg. Waller says that the victims really were dancing. They were not just shaking or moving strangely. But the dancers were not having fun. In fact, they were very **frightened**. They were suffering **terribly**. So why were they dancing? And why
10   couldn't they stop?

The strange events of 1518, known as the Dancing Plague, are an example of mass psychogenic illness. *Mass* means a large number. *Psychogenic* means coming from the mind. Mass psychogenic illness usually appears when many people are living in a terrible situation for a long time. They begin to feel **desperate**. Then a
15   few people begin to behave strangely. For example, they start moving in a strange way, or they start laughing and can't stop. The behavior quickly **spreads** from one person to another, like a fever. Soon almost everyone in the community is suffering. It can take days, weeks, or months for victims to come to their senses.

There is no physical cause of mass psychogenic illness. However, there are often
20   physical results. People who are suffering from mass psychogenic illness do not feel that they are in control of their own actions.

Waller says that the conditions in Strasbourg in 1518 were perfect for mass psychogenic illness. Unusual weather, such as hot, dry summers and very cold winters, had killed all of the **crops**. Many people were dying of hunger. At the
25   same time, deadly illnesses such as smallpox[4] were killing thousands of people. The situation was desperate.

But why did the illness take the form of dancing? People of that time were very superstitious. Most ordinary people believed in **spirits** that had the power to punish them. And one of the punishments was an uncontrollable dance.
30   The Dancing Plague is just one example of mass psychogenic illness in history. Similar events have happened all over the world. And mass psychogenic illness is not just a thing of the past. Recently, a group of twenty students fainted[5] in a schoolroom in Tanzania. No physical cause was found. At the time, the students were preparing for important exams. They were under a lot of pressure. Experts
35   believe that the cause of the fainting was mass psychogenic illness.

---

[1] **heart attack:** a serious medical condition in which a person's heart suddenly stops working

[2] **stroke:** a sudden illness in which a tube carrying blood in your brain bursts or becomes blocked

[3] **exhaustion:** being extremely tired

[4] **smallpox:** a serious disease that causes spots on a person's skin

[5] **faint:** become unconscious for a short time

Vocabulary Check

Write the target word from the list on page 178 next to the correct definition.

1. _____ = very many (more than twelve)

2. _____ = willing to do anything to change a very bad situation

3. _____ = a thing like a person, but which does not have a physical body, such as a ghost

4. _____ = someone who studies important past events

5. _____ = to get bigger by having an effect on a larger area

6. _____ = a plant such as corn, fruit, etc. that a farmer grows

7. _____ = in a very serious and bad way

8. _____ = to feel pain or the effects of a sickness

9. _____ = feeling afraid

> READ AGAIN

Read "The Dancing Plague" again and complete the comprehension exercises on the next page. As you work, keep the reading goal in mind.

> **READING GOAL:** To identify an example of mass psychogenic illness

Comprehension Check

A. Circle the letter of the correct answer to complete each sentence.

1. "The Dancing Plague" is about a group of people living through a(n) _____ experience.
   a. difficult   **b.** interesting

2. Many people in the group feel _____.
   a. desperate   **b.** in control

3. One person in the group starts to _____.
   a. do something strange   **b.** come to his or her senses

4. The person _____ in control of his/her own actions or feelings.
   a. is   **b.** is not

5. Others in the group start to feel or do _____.
   a. the same thing   **b.** something different

6. The behavior or feeling _____.
   a. spreads   **b.** begins

7. The behavior or feeling is sometimes _____.
   a. fun   **b.** dangerous

8. There isn't a real physical _____ of the feeling or behavior.
   a. cause   **b.** result

B. Read the three descriptions. Check (✓) the one that is an example of mass psychogenic illness. Use the information in the reading and in Exercise A to help you decide.

_____ **1.** Some popular high school students decide to wear hats to class every day. After a few days, other students start wearing hats, too. Soon, all of the students in the school are wearing hats. After a few months, one student decides not to wear a hat. The next day, no one in the school wears a hat.

_____ **2.** An airplane with fifty people on it crashes. Everyone survives, but they are lost in the mountains. One of them becomes ill after drinking dirty water from the river. Soon, all of them are ill from the dirty water. They don't think they will survive. They feel desperate. Finally, after ten days, they are found. For many years, they have nightmares (bad dreams) about their terrible experience.

(continued on next page)

_____ **3.** There is a terrible earthquake in a small town. Many people die. Schools are closed for a month. The day the schools open again, a teacher feels the ground shaking. Her students feel it, too. They run outside. Students from other classes follow them. Several students fall down and get hurt. Everyone is crying and screaming, "It's an earthquake!" Experts say that there was no earthquake, but the teachers and students don't believe them. They feel the shaking for several days. Many families leave the town.

C. Work with a partner. Explain your answers for Exercise B. Use the information in Exercise A when you explain the reason for your answer.

> DISCUSS

Work in small groups. Ask and answer the questions.

1. Do you think the people in Holland during the time of "tulip fever" were suffering from mass psychogenic illness? Why or why not?

2. Do you know of any other cases of mass psychogenic illness? If so, tell your group.

> VOCABULARY SKILL BUILDING

Vocabulary Skill: Adjectives and Adverbs

In Chapter 3, you learned that *adjectives* describe nouns. Adjectives often come in front of nouns and answer the question "What kind of [noun]?"

EXAMPLE:

What kind of question did he ask? *He asked a <u>serious</u> question.*

↓

adjective

Adverbs describe verbs. Many adverbs are formed by adding the suffix *-ly* to the adjective. Adverbs often come after the verb and answer the question "How?" or "In what way?"

EXAMPLE:

How (In what way) did she answer? *She answered <u>seriously</u>.*

↓

adverb

A. Complete the sentences. Circle the correct form of the underlined words.

1. They were suffering terrible / terribly.

2. Their strange / strangely behavior was frightening.

3. She answered fearful / fearfully.

4. They arrived together, but they left separate / separately.

5. He's the best student in the class. He always participates active / actively.

6. He doesn't have any free time because he gives his full / fully attention to his studies.

7. They were dancing wild / wildly through the streets.

8. No one heard his desperate / desperately cries for help.

B. Put the words in their correct order to make sentences. Use a capital letter for the first word in the sentence. Put a period at the end.

1. is / she / an / girl / ordinary

   She is an ordinary girl.

2. hands / her / wildly / shook

   _____

3. his / mistake / he / for / terrible / apologized

   _____

4. were / thinking / they / clearly / not

   _____

5. suffering / she / from / terrible / a / illness / is

   _____

6. spread / the / quickly / fever

   _____

7. cry / children / started / frightened / the / to

   _____

Learn the Vocabulary

Choosing Words to Learn

There are many words in English. You should learn the most frequent words first. That is why it is important to know how frequent a word is before you learn it. There are two places where you can find information about word frequency: a good English/English dictionary and the Internet. Every dictionary shows frequency differently, so you will need to read the guide at the beginning of your dictionary.

To find information about word frequency on the Internet, go online and type the keywords "word frequency" and "English" in the search box, or ask your teacher for help.

Some of the Web sites have lists of the most frequent words in English. Some of them have a place where you can enter a word, a paragraph, or a whole text into a program. Then the program will "read" your text and give you information about the frequency level of the word(s).

If the word you checked has a high frequency level, make a word card for it right away. If its frequency level is not very high, don't make a card for it until you have seen it two more times.

A. For two or three days, make a list of words that you do not know. Include target words, words that you wrote on page 192, and any other new words. Then check the frequency of each of the words. Use an English/ English dictionary or the Internet.

B. Decide which words you should learn first, based on their frequency. Make cards for the words you choose.

C. Report back to your class on which of the words (from Exercise A) you decided to learn and why. In the future, follow these suggestions whenever you are deciding whether or not to learn a new word.

D. Go back to the vocabulary list at the beginning of each chapter. What did you learn about the target words? Add your numbers to the lists.

Vocabulary Practice 12, see page 204

FLUENCY PRACTICE 4

Fluency Strategy

To become a more fluent reader, you need to read every day, and you need to read a lot. The material should be very easy for you, but you need to read many pages a week. Ask your teacher to help you find readings that are at the correct level. Graded readers—books that have been written with a simple vocabulary—are a good place to start. Again, your teacher can help you to find readers at the correct level. Set yourself a goal of a certain number of pages every week. For example, you can start by reading 25 pages a week. Then increase the number of pages by ten pages every week, so that in the second week you are reading 35 pages, 45 in the third week, and so on.

> READING 1

Before You Read

Scan "Twins in the News" on the next page and answer the questions.

1. What are the names of the twins in the article?

   _____

2. Who is Ruth Reichl?

   _____

3. What kind of business did Debbie and Lisa have in 1995?

   _____

4. What kind of business do they have today?

   _____

Read

A. Read "Twins in the News." Time yourself. Write your start and end times and your total reading time. Then calculate your reading speed (words per minute) and write it in the progress chart on page 205.

Start time: _____   **End time:** _____   **Total time:** _____ (in seconds)

Reading speed:
334 words ÷ _____ (total time in seconds) x 60 = _____ words per minute

TWINS IN THE NEWS

1　Hello! We are identical twin sisters. We started this blog because so many people are interested in twins. It appears that people never get tired of hearing about us! The news

5　is full of stories about twins. We collect these stories and post them on our blog. We hope you will find them interesting!

Debbie and Lisa Ganz

Debbie and Lisa Ganz are identical twins.

10　They are also successful businesswomen. In 1994, they opened a restaurant in New York City called Twins. All of the servers in the restaurant were identical twins. They always worked the same hours. If one of

15　the twins was ill, the other one had to stay home, too. If one twin quit, the other twin also had to leave. Many of the restaurant's customers were also twins. Twins all over the world heard about the restaurant and wanted

20　to visit it. Ruth Reichl, a famous restaurant writer, wrote this about the restaurant in *The New York Times* in 1995:

> *"Twins, owned by one pair of twins and staffed by many others, creates its own…*
> 25　*world of doubles. Most times there are twins at some of the tables as well, which makes those of us who came into the world alone feel as if we were somehow cheated. Where are our doubles?"*

30　The restaurant is closed now, but Debbie and Lisa have another successful business. They own a talent agency. The agency specializes in twins. They find work for twins in movies, television commercials, advertisements, and

35　reality shows. Child actors who are twins have a special advantage. There are laws to protect children who work. As a result, most child actors can work for only a few hours a day. But child actors who are twins can share

40　one job. This doubles the work that they can complete in one day. Mary-Kate and Ashley Olsen are a very famous example of this. At just nine months old, they began to play one character on the popular television show

45　*Full House.*

B. Read "Twins in the News" again, a little faster this time. Write your start and end times and your total reading time. Then calculate your reading speed (words per minute) and write it in the progress chart on page 205.

Start time: _____　　**End time:** _____　　**Total time:** _____ (in seconds)

Reading speed:
334 words ÷ _____ (total time in seconds) x 60 = _____ words per minute

Comprehension Check

A. Answer the questions.

1. Who are the writers of the blog?
2. What kinds of stories can you find on the blog?
3. Who might be interested in reading this blog?
4. How was Debbie and Lisa Ganz's restaurant different from other restaurants?
5. How is their talent agency different from other talent agencies?

B. Complete the paragraph with the words from the list. Try not to look back at the reading.

agency	famous	owned	successful
character	identical	special	

    Debbie and Lisa Ganz are (1)_____ twins. They are also

(2)_____ businesswomen. From 1994 to 1996, they

(3)_____ a restaurant in New York City called Twins. Today,

they have a talent (4)_____. They find work for actors. Many

of the actors are twins. Child actors who are twins have a

(5)_____ advantage. They can play one (6)_____

on a television show. The Olsen twins are one famous example. They

played the same little girl on the (7)_____ television show

Full House.

C. Check your answers for the comprehension questions in the Answer Key on page 206. Then calculate your score and write it in the progress chart on page 205.

_____ (my number correct) ÷ 12 x 100 = _____%

→ READING 2

Before You Read

A. Read the definition of *miracle*. You will see this word in the reading.

> **miracle:** a very unusual event that has no logical or scientific explanation

B. Preview "The Miracle Twins" and answer the questions.

1. Where did this reading come from?
   a. Lisa and Debbie Ganz's blog
   b. a magazine about Miracle
   c. an Ecuadorian newspaper

2. Why are the girls called "the miracle twins"?
   a. They almost died when they were born.
   b. Their mother didn't know that she was having twins.
   c. They found each other by chance.

Read

A. Read "The Miracle Twins." Time yourself. Write your start and end times and your total reading time. Then calculate your reading speed (words per minute) and write it in the progress chart on page 205.

Start time: _____   **End time:** _____   **Total time:** _____ (in seconds)

Reading speed:
575 words ÷ _____ (total time in seconds) x 60 = _____ words per minute

http://www.ganztwins.com/miracletwins/

THE MIRACLE TWINS

1 Imagine this: You are in a town called Miracle. You are at a restaurant with your fourteen-year-old daughter. Suddenly, you see a girl walking toward you. But she is no ordinary
5 girl. You think there is a problem with your eyes. Maybe you are seeing double? But no, this is real. The girl looks shockingly like your daughter. In fact, she is a perfect copy of her! No, this is not a movie. It is a true story. It
10 really happened to Petita Penaherrera of Ecuador, South America. She and her daughter Andrea were in a restaurant in

Milagro (Spanish for "miracle") in southern Ecuador when they ran into a girl who was

15 identical to Andrea. The girl, Marielisa, was with her parents, Roberto Romo and Isabel Garcia. They are both doctors. In fact, they were Penaherrera's doctors when her daughter Andrea was born. Andrea and

20 Marielisa are identical twins.

Everyone agrees that this part of the story is true. But there are still many questions. Why were Andrea and her identical twin separated? Did the doctors hide Marielisa's

25 true identity from her real parents? If so, why? The two families live in the same city. Why didn't the two girls run into each other earlier?

Not surprisingly, Penaherrera's story is very different from the doctors' story. There were

30 problems with the birth, so Penaherrera wasn't awake when the babies were born. Penaherrera says that she never knew that she was having twins. Why not? She says the doctors never told her. "They stole her

35 from me, the doctors stole my daughter," Penaherrera says.

Penaherrera and her husband have accused Romo and Garcia of taking their daughter illegally and then hiding her true identify

40 for years. They say that the doctors lied to officials. They signed papers saying that Mariesela was their own child.

The doctors tell a very different story. Dr. Garcia told a reporter, "The nurse

45 said…, 'Congratulations you have two girls'…The woman just cried and cried."

Penaherrera was only sixteen years old at the time. Garcia says that the teenager was desperate. She was young, frightened, and

50 alone. Penaherrera and her husband were separated at the time. She did not have any financial help. When she left the clinic, she took only one of the girls. She left the other one behind. She never came back for her.

55 The doctors then kept the girl. Their lawyers say they did it to protect the child. They also say that Penaherrera and her husband are just trying to get money from Romo and Garcia.

60 It is a difficult case. Many of the facts are not clear. After fifteen years, witnesses' memories can't always be trusted. The court will probably take a long time to make a decision.

How do the girls feel about all of this? At

65 first they were very happy to find each other. However, the pressure on both of them is terrible. People recognize them everywhere they go. Marielisa is probably suffering the most. She wants Penaherrera to stop the

70 legal action. She says Romo and Garcia were good parents. She wants to remain with them. But Penaherrera and her husband don't think that their daughters should live apart. And they don't want Marielisa to

75 remain with people they say are guilty of a terrible crime.

> What's your opinion? Was what happened in Milagro really a miracle? Or was it a disaster? Let us know what you think.

80 ☞ Post a comment

B. Read "The Miracle Twins" again, a little faster this time. Write your start and end times and your total reading time. Then calculate your reading speed (words per minute) and write it in the progress chart on page 205.

Start time: _____   End time: _____   Total time: _____ (in seconds)

Reading speed:
575 words ÷ _____ (total time in seconds) x 60 = _____ words per minute

C. Check your answers to the Before You Read questions on page 188. Are they correct? If not, correct them.

Comprehension Check

A. Circle the letter of the correct answer to complete each sentence.

1. Marielisa and Andrea _____.
   a. were raised by different parents
   b. are different ages
   c. have the same last name

2. They met each other when they were _____.
   a. at the doctors' clinic
   b. teenagers
   c. fifteen years old

3. Andrea was raised by _____.
   a. her biological parents
   b. her mother's doctors
   c. Garcia and Romo

4. Marielisa lives with _____.
   a. her biological parents
   b. two doctors
   c. Petita Penaherrera

5. Andrea's mother and father say that _____.
   a. the doctors stole Marielisa from them
   b. they took Marielisa to protect her
   c. Marielisa should remain with the doctors

6. Romo and Garcia say that Petita Penaherrera _____.
   a. was never their patient
   b. didn't want to keep Marielisa
   c. is a liar and a criminal

B. What do you think? Is Marielisa and Andrea's story a miracle, or is it a disaster? Should Romo and Garcia be punished? Write a comment on the blog. Explain your answers.

C. Check your answers for the comprehension questions in the Answer Key on page 206. Then calculate your score and write it in the progress chart on page 205.

_____ (my number correct) ÷ 6 x 100 = _____%

New Words

UNIT 1

UNIT 2

UNIT 3

UNIT 4

UNIT 5

UNIT 6

New Words

UNIT 7

UNIT 8

UNIT 9

UNIT 10

UNIT 11

UNIT 12

THINK ABOUT MEANING

Read the questions and answers. Two of the answers are correct, but one is incorrect. Cross out the incorrect answer. The boldfaced words are the target words.

1. What can you **burn**?   calories / trees / ~~water~~

2. What can you **win**?   medals / games / waves

3. What do you need **energy** for?   to exercise / to see / to move forward

4. Where are there **waves**?   in the house / in the water / on the beach

5. What is a way to **exercise**?   swimming / eating / running

6. What is an **advantage** when you are looking for a job?   experience / land / training

7. What makes you feel **relaxed**?   a hot bath / exercise / flat feet

8. What is **natural**?   a house / the land / an animal

9. What is a part of the **body**?   land / foot / shoulder

10. What can you **kick**?   a ball / energy / a chair

PRACTICE A SKILL: Parts of Speech

Read the sentences. Are the underlined words nouns, verbs, or adjectives? Write *N*, *V*, or *A*.

_____ 1. How much do you weigh?

_____ 2. She's in the hospital. A horse kicked her.

_____ 3. Don't worry. It's safe.

_____ 4. Today is a special day.

_____ 5. Look at the surface of the water.

_____ 6. I feel very relaxed.

_____ 7. The waves are powerful today.

_____ 8. I always stretch before I exercise.

PRACTICE A STRATEGY: Using Word Cards

Make word cards for 10 more words that you learn this week. Add them to the cards that you made for this unit. Review your cards every day. Always change the order of your cards before you review them.

VOCABULARY PRACTICE 2

THINK ABOUT MEANING

Look at each group of words. Cross out the one word or phrase in each group that does not belong.

1. lie	trick	~~pocket~~
2. wear	remove	follow
3. clever	special	the same
4. shoulder	meal	body
5. water	wave	grass
6. followed	punished	ashamed
7. jacket	pocket	meal
8. stretch	exercise	share
9. bottom	burn	surface
10. ashamed	apologize	win

PRACTICE A SKILL: Parts of Speech

Read the sentences. Are the <u>underlined</u> words nouns, verbs, or adjectives? Write *N*, *V*, or *A*.

_____ **1.** That is a very <u>tricky</u> question. I am not sure of the answer.

_____ **2.** Children sometimes like to play <u>tricks</u> on their teachers.

_____ **3.** I don't have any <u>pockets</u>. Can you put my keys in your bag?

_____ **4.** He didn't give me any money. He <u>pocketed</u> it.

_____ **5.** Their mother <u>punished</u> them because they lied to her.

_____ **6.** What was their <u>punishment</u>?

_____ **7.** Please wash your hands. They're <u>dirty</u>.

_____ **8.** You can't wear that shirt. It has <u>dirt</u> on it.

_____ **9.** The <u>grass</u> is green.

_____ **10.** Let's find a <u>grassy</u> place to sit down.

PRACTICE A STRATEGY: Using Word Cards

Review your cards every day. If you remember a word correctly three times, remove that card and put it away in a safe place. (Don't throw it away!) Then after a few days, put that card back with the other cards, change the order, and review all of your cards again.

THINK ABOUT MEANING

Look at the words in the list. Think about their meanings, and decide where to put them in the chart. Some of the words can go in more than one place in the chart. Be ready to explain your decisions.

Food	Training	Danger
		death

death	prepare
full	raw
license	responsible
pass	serious
poisonous	survive
practical	wild

PRACTICE A SKILL: Word Families

Look at the words in the chart. If the word doesn't have a suffix, put an *X* in the chart. If the word has a suffix, write the suffix in the second column. Then remove the suffix to make another word in the same word family. Make sure you spell the new word correctly.

Word	Suffix	Word without the suffix
1. agreement	-ment	agree
2. full	X	X
3. ground		
4. imagination		
5. scientist		
6. raw		
7. pass		
8. license		
9. dangerous		
10. poison		
11. preparation		
12. death		

PRACTICE A STRATEGY: Using Word Cards with Example Sentences

Review your word cards for this unit. If a word is difficult for you to remember, add an example sentence to the back of the card. You can copy the sentence from the reading, or you can copy an example sentence from your dictionary.

THINK ABOUT MEANING

Look at the words and phrases in the list. Think about their meanings and decide where to put them in the chart. Be ready to explain your decisions.

brain	find out	humorous	popular	speech
experiment	fun	interpreter	physical	translate

Body:	*brain*
Science:	
Language:	
Good time:	

PRACTICE A SKILL: Suffixes

Add the suffixes from the list to the words. Make at least one new form of each word. For some of the words, it is possible to make more than one new form. Be careful. You might need to change the spelling when you add the suffix.

Adjective suffixes	Noun suffixes	
-al, -ous	*-er*, *-or* (person)	*-ity*, *-tion* (thing or idea)

1. interpret — *interpreter, interpretation* _____
2. translate — _____
3. similar — _____
4. experiment — _____
5. emotion — _____
6. active — _____
7. humor — _____

PRACTICE A STRATEGY: Using a Dictionary

A. Use your dictionary to check your answers to Practice a Skill. Correct any spelling mistakes.

B. Now check the pronunciation for each word. Which syllable is stressed? Circle the stressed syllable in each word in Practice a Skill.

VOCABULARY PRACTICE 5

THINK ABOUT MEANING

Complete the sentences with the words from the list. The boldfaced words are the target words. Be careful. There are four extra words.

alone	body	famous	follow	owner
apologize	each other	fashionable	license	safe

1. You don't need a _____ to **ride** in a car, but you need one to drive.

2. If you don't **treat** someone well, you should _____.

3. When two people are **strangers**, they don't know _____.

4. I **feel sorry for** old people who live _____.

5. If you can't **identify** a wild mushroom, it isn't _____ to eat it.

6. If nobody **recognizes** you, you are probably not very _____.

PRACTICE A SKILL: The prefix *dis-*

Write the letter of the correct definition next to the word.

_____ **1.** disability   **a.** become impossible to see or find

_____ **2.** disagree   **b.** a physical or mental condition that makes it difficult for someone to do things

_____ **3.** disown   **c.** have a different opinion from someone else

_____ **4.** disadvantage   **d.** not the same

_____ **5.** dissimilar   **e.** a bad feature or characteristic of something

_____ **6.** disappear   **f.** end your relationship with your own child

PRACTICE A STRATEGY: Using a Dictionary

Use an English/English dictionary to find answers to the questions.

1. **a.** How many syllables are there in **recognize**? _____

   b. Which syllable is stressed? _____

2. What word should you look up to find a definition of **feel sorry for**? _____

3. **a.** How is the first *c* of **accept** pronounced? _____

   b. How is the second *c* pronounced? _____

4. **a.** What do you **ride** *in*? _*a car,*_____

   b. What do you **ride** *on*? _____

VOCABULARY PRACTICE 6

THINK ABOUT MEANING

Circle the letter of the correct answer to complete each sentence. The boldfaced words are the target words.

1. **Efficient** people are usually _____.
   a. ill   b. organized   c. slow

2. An **intelligent** person is _____.
   a. clever   b. dangerous   c. disorganized

3. An **illness** makes you _____.
   a. intelligent b. safe   c. sick

4. We **solved** _____.
   a. a problem   b. buildings   c. him

5. I don't want to _____. Let's try to be friends.
   a. agree   b. apologize   c. fight

6. Did you **collect** the _____?
   a. evolution   b. fashion   c. tickets

7. I got wet because I walked _____.
   a. without an umbrella   b. on the **path**   c. forward

8. They **protected** her, so she felt _____.
   a. alone   b. safe   c. pressure

PRACTICE A SKILL: Collocations

A. Complete the sentences with the correct collocations for the boldfaced words. If you can't remember the collocations, look up the boldfaced words in your dictionary.

1. When you play a game, you need to _____ **the rules**.

2. You can't do that! It's _____ **the rules**!

3. You look ill. Let me _____ your **temperature**.

4. Wear a warm coat. The **temperature** is going to _____ tonight.

B. Read the definitions. Then look up the boldfaced words in your dictionary, and write the correct word(s) to complete each collocation.

Definition	Collocation
1. do something without knowing what will happen after you do it	_____ a **chance**
2. several days of very hot weather	a **heat** _____
3. have a fight with someone	_____ _____ a **fight**

PRACTICE A STRATEGY: Using Word Cards for Collocations

Make a word card for each of the collocations in Practice a Skill, Exercises A and B. Write the collocation on one side of the card and the definition or translation on the other side.

THINK ABOUT MEANING

Circle the letter of the correct answer to complete each sentence. The boldfaced words are the target words.

1. Use a **mirror** to check _____.

    a. your hair   **b.** an exercise   **c.** a prediction

2. They listened to the **warning**, so they _____.

    a. survived   **b.** died   **c.** guessed

3. She prepared everything **in advance**, so she _____.

    a. could relax   **b.** didn't finish   **c.** was nervous

4. Luckily when the storm **hit** we _____.

    a. felt good   **b.** were safe   **c.** hunted

5. I just felt a **drop** of water. I'm going to take _____.

    a. a shower   **b.** an umbrella   **c.** a walk

6. She has a great **mind**. She is _____.

    a. clever   **b.** nervous   **c.** pretty

7. The **opposite** of **alive** is _____.

    a. dead   **b.** living   **c.** luck

8. That is **nonsense**. You should _____ it.

    a. believe   **b.** not listen to   **c.** predict

PRACTICE A SKILL: Nouns that End in *-ing*

Read the paragraph. Are the boldfaced words gerunds or verbs? Circle the gerunds, and underline the verbs.

Do you think that **hunting** is wrong? Some people think that **hunting** for food is acceptable, but causing death for fun is wrong. For other people, **killing** animals is always wrong, so they stop **eating** meat and become vegetarians. But is the number of vegetarians in the world **growing**? No one really knows. In the United States and many other countries, people are **eating** more meat today than at any time in the past.

PRACTICE A STRATEGY: Finding Members of the Same Word Family

First circle the part of speech (**adjective, noun, verb**) that is missing in the sentences. Then complete the sentences with the correct form of the words from the list.

opposition	predict	storm	superstitious

1. I'm not (*adj./n.*) _____. I don't believe in bad luck.

2. There is a lot of (*adj./n.*) _____ to your plan. Many people dislike it.

3. We live on (*adj./n.*) _____ sides of the same street.

4. It was a very (*adj./n.*) _____ day, with a lot of rain and wind.

5. You said that they would win, and they did. Your (*v./n.*) _____ was correct.

6. Nobody can (*v./n.*) _____ the weather a month in advance.

VOCABULARY PRACTICE 8

THINK ABOUT MEANING

Look at the words in the list. Circle the words that have a positive meaning (something good), and underline the words that have a negative meaning (something bad).

community	disaster	hold on	security	trapped
crash	fear	independent	skilled	trust

PRACTICE A SKILL: Prefixes and Suffixes

Look at the words in the chart. Write the prefixes and suffixes in the correct columns. If a word does not have a prefix or a suffix, put an *X* in that column. Be careful. Some of the words do not have a prefix or a suffix, and some have both.

Word	Prefix	Suffix
1. fearful	*X*	*-ful*
2. fearless		
3. disastrous		
4. independent		
5. dependable		
6. insecure		
7. distrust		
8. instead		

PRACTICE A STRATEGY: Figuring Out Meaning from Context

Read the sentences. The boldfaced words are related to target words from the unit. Can you guess their meanings? Underline the words that help you understand the meaning. Then check your answers in a dictionary.

1. He loves to take risks, and he never worries about getting hurt. He is **fearless**.

   Fearless means _____.

2. She is **fearful** of everything. Because of her fears, she cannot live an independent life.

   Fearful means _____.

3. I had a **disastrous** day. Everything went wrong. I just want to go home and go to bed!

   Disastrous means _____.

4. I have no reason to **distrust** him. He has always been honest with me.

   Distrust means _____.

THINK ABOUT MEANING

Complete the sentences with the words from the list. The boldfaced words are the target words. Be careful. There are six extra words.

bury	condition	expert	identity	professional	sneak
cash	crime	fool	nest	release	steal

1. He is an excellent **lawyer**. He is an _____ in **criminal** law.

2. He has **financial** problems. The bank will not _____ any of his checks.

3. The police will not _____ him because they think he will **run away** again.

4. She has had a very **successful career** as a _____ musician.

5. He **pretends** to be an **expert**, but he has no training. He tries to _____ everyone.

6. They plan to _____ into the museum and **steal** the painting.

PRACTICE A SKILL: Collocations

A. Complete each collocation with a word from the list. Be careful. There are two extra words.

career	crime	fool	nest	sneak	steal

1. When you **commit** a _____, there is always the risk that the police will catch you.

2. He's a _____ **criminal**. He has been in and out of prison and has never had a real job.

3. The movie will not be in theaters until May, but there is a _____ **preview** tonight.

4. When my husband lost his job, we spent our savings. Now we don't have a _____ **egg**.

B. Write the collocations from Exercise A next to the correct definitions.

1. do something illegal such as robbing a bank _____

2. money that people save for their old age _____

3. a person who is a criminal his/her whole life _____

4. a chance to see or experience something before anyone else _____

PRACTICE A STRATEGY: Using Word Cards to Learn Collocations

Make a word card for each of the collocations from Practice a Skill. Write the collocation on one side of the card. On the other side, write the meaning and an example sentence.

VOCABULARY PRACTICE 10

THINK ABOUT MEANING

Circle the letter of the correct answer to complete each sentence. The boldfaced words are the target words.

1. When you **run into** someone, you meet that person _____.
   a. alone　　**b. apart**　　**c.** by chance

2. Those two pictures are **identical**. They are _____.
   a. copies　　**b.** different　　**c. legal**

3. Your **knees** are a part of your _____.
   a. body　　**b.** mind　　**c.** style

4. I like to have **company**. I don't like to be _____.
   a. alone　　**b.** ashamed　　**c. shocked**

5. I'm tired. I want to _____.
   a. lie down　　**b.** have **company**　　**c. run into** a friend

6. Twins often wear _____ clothes.
   a. legal　　**b. matching**　　**c.** opposite

7. I wear a raincoat _____ it rains.
   a. except　　**b. in case**　　**c. unless**

8. Newspapers **publish** _____.
   a. the news　　**b. agencies**　　**c. company**

PRACTICE A SKILL: Word Families

The words in the list are in the same word families as some of the target words from the unit. Complete the sentences with the words.

Nouns:	shock	inspection	publication
Verbs:	accompany	match	separate

1. A magazine is an example of one kind of _____. Other examples include books and newspapers.

2. It was a _____ to hear that he was in the hospital.

3. Before you buy a house, you should always get a home _____. That way you will know if there are any problems with the house.

4. Your shoes don't _____ your dress. Do you have any other shoes?

5. Can you _____ me to the doctor? I don't want to go alone.

6. Please _____ the light-colored clothes from the dark ones before you wash them.

PRACTICE A STRATEGY: Using Word Cards

Add the word forms from Practice a Skill to the cards you made for the target words. On the back of the card, add one example sentence for each word form. Leave a blank for the word. When you review the cards, look at the sentences and try to remember the correct word form for each sentence.

THINK ABOUT MEANING

Circle the letter of the correct answer to complete each sentence. The boldfaced words are the target words.

1. You feel **guilty** when you _____.
   a. steal something
   b. help someone
   c. are a victim of a crime

2. If you have poor **sight**, you _____.
   a. can't taste your food
   b. can't hear
   c. need glasses

3. If you **touch** a hot stove, it will _____.
   a. cook your food
   b. hurt
   c. smell

4. She's the **victim**. Everyone feels _____.
   a. ashamed of her
   b. relaxed around her
   c. sorry for her

5. We **clap** with our _____.
   a. hands
   b. knees
   c. shoulders

6. It is a **secret**. Nobody _____ it.
   a. knows about
   b. listens to
   c. understands

7. The lights are **bright**. _____.
   a. Please turn them on
   b. They hurt my eyes
   c. I can't read

8. We have to **remain** here. We can't _____.
   a. leave
   b. stay
   c. touch

PRACTICE A SKILL: Roots and Prefixes

Complete the words in the sentences with a prefix or a stem from the list.

Prefixes:	co-	inter-	pre-	trans-
Roots:	-dic-	-memor-	-spect-	-vis-

1. A/An _____able event is an event that you are able to remember because it was special.

2. A/An _____acular sunset is a beautiful sunset that everyone wants to see.

3. The _____pilot sits next to the pilot of an airplane and works together with the pilot.

4. The marriage between an African-American man and a Chinese woman is a/an _____racial marriage.

6. Someone with good _____tion speaks very clearly and pronounces every sound carefully.

7. A special hat that protects your eyes from the sun is called a/an _____or.

8. When you fly across the Atlantic Ocean, you are making a/an _____atlantic trip.

PRACTICE A STRATEGY: Using a Dictionary and Making Word Cards

Check your answers to Practice a Skill in your dictionary. Then make a word card for each of the new words.

THINK ABOUT MEANING

Look at each group of words. Cross out the one word in each group that does not belong.

1. illness   fever   wealth
2. desperate   humorous   terrible
3. crop   farmer   sight
4. cash   wealth   spirit
5. ordinary   special   unusual
6. gardener   image   land
7. frightened   nervous   secure
8. hurt   publish   suffer
9. historian   expert   thief
10. agency   double   dozen

PRACTICE A SKILL: Parts of Speech

Circle the correct word (noun, adjective, or adverb) to complete each sentence.

1. She smiled nervousness / nervous / nervously.
2. He cried out desperation / desperate / desperately for help.
3. World War I and II were historian / historic / historically events.
4. He is a fear / fearful / fearfully child.
5. They live in separation / separate / separately houses.
6. He was a wealthy man, but he spent his money fool / foolish / foolishly.
7. You should never touch a wildness / wild / wildly animal.
8. My hands always shake when I am nervousness / nervous / nervously.
9. You don't need to pretend. Just behave nature / natural / naturally.
10. People sometimes do strangeness / strange / strangely things when they are frightened.

PRACTICE A STRATEGY: Choosing Words to Learn

Use an English/English dictionary. Circle the word in each set that is used more frequently.

1. borrow   crop   6. spread   tulip
2. desperate   dozen   7. garden   gardener
3. farmer   fever   8. history   historian
4. frightened   market   9. worth   worthless
5. ordinary   spirit   10. shake   shaky

Fluency Progress Charts

FLUENCY PRACTICE 1

	Words per Minute	
	First Try	Second Try
Reading 1		
Reading 2		
Comprehension Check Score _____ %		

FLUENCY PRACTICE 2

	Words per Minute	
	First Try	Second Try
Reading 1		
Reading 2		
Comprehension Check Score _____ %		

FLUENCY PRACTICE 3

	Words per Minute	
	First Try	Second Try
Reading 1		
Reading 2		
Comprehension Check Score _____ %		

FLUENCY PRACTICE 4

	Words per Minute	
	First Try	Second Try
Reading 1		
Reading 2		
Comprehension Check Score _____ %		

Fluency Practice Answer Key

Count only the Comprehension Check answers (not the Read answers) toward your Comprehension Check Score.

Fluency Practice 1
Reading 1
Comprehension Check, p. 43

A.

1. a **2.** a **3.** c **4.** c

B.

1. happy **2.** hair **3.** Christmas
4. money **5.** sell **6.** buy **7.** Jim

Reading 2
Read, p. 45

C. *Answers may vary but should include the following:*

1. Della will sell her hair.
2. Della will buy a gift for Jim.

Comprehension Check, p. 45

A.

1. b **2.** a **3.** c **4.** a **5.** a

B.

1. 3

Fluency Practice 2
Reading 1
Comprehension Check, p. 91

A.

1. F **2.** T **3.** T **4.** T **5.** F **6.** T
7. F **8.** F **9.** T **10.** T **11.** T

B.

1. baby duckling **2.** Pinky
3. their house **4.** healthy, hungry duck with white feathers **5.** upstairs and downstairs OR everywhere OR all over
6. take baths **7.** treated **8.** parents
9. other ducks **10.** park **11.** two miles
12. other ducks **13.** sad **14.** visit

Reading 2
Read, p. 93

C. *Answers may vary but should include the following:*

1. Pinky does not get along with the other ducks.

2. Sara gets Pinky back.

Comprehension Check, p. 93

A.

1. c **2.** c **3.** c **4.** a **5.** a **6.** b **7.** b

Fluency Practice 3
Reading 1
Comprehension Check, p. 140

A.

1. c **2.** b **3.** b **4.** b **5.** a

B.

1. English teacher **2.** other cultures
3. a collection of superstitions from all over the world OR a book **4.** post information about superstitions in their countries **5.** collect the superstitions
6. publisher **7.** donate the money (to an organization that works to form better understanding among cultures)

Reading 2
Read, p. 143

C.

1. South Korea and Russia
2. Sungho studied English in Scotland and was there for New Year's Eve.
3. Elena
4. b, d, e, f

Comprehension Check, p. 143

A.

1 and **2.** *Answers may vary:* look at a newborn baby, say anything nice about a baby, break a mirror, look in a broken mirror, eat and drink while looking in a mirror

3. have to go home for something you forgot
4. look in a mirror before you leave the house again
5. don't wash your hair
6. your memories will be washed away
7. give a boyfriend or girlfriend a pair of shoes
8. he or she will walk away and leave you all alone
9. the first person to come to your house in a new year
10. leave your house before someone has visited you
11. tall, black-haired men
12. females with red hair

Fluency Practice 4
Reading 1
Comprehension Check, p. 187

A.

1. Debbie and Lisa Ganz, identical twin sisters
2. stories about twins
3. twins and other people interested in twins
4. All of the servers were identical twins.
5. The agency specializes in twins.

B.

1. identical **2.** successful **3.** owned
4. agency **5.** special **6.** character
7. popular

Reading 2
Read, p. 190

C.

1. a **2.** c

Comprehension Check, p. 190

A.

1. a **2.** b **3.** a **4.** b **5.** a **6.** b

B. *Answers will vary.* (Do not count toward Comprehension Check Score.)

Pronunciation Table

Vowels

Symbol	Key Word
i	b**ea**t, f**ee**d
ɪ	b**i**t, d**i**d
eɪ	d**a**te, p**ai**d
ɛ	b**e**t, b**e**d
æ	b**a**t, b**a**d
ɑ	b**o**x, **o**dd, f**a**ther
ɔ	b**ough**t, d**o**g
oʊ	b**oa**t, r**oa**d
ʊ	b**oo**k, g**oo**d
u	b**oo**t, f**oo**d, st**u**dent
ʌ	b**u**t, m**u**d, m**o**ther
ə	b**a**n**a**n**a**, **a**moung
ɚ	sh**ir**t, m**ur**d**er**
aɪ	b**i**te, c**r**y, b**u**y, **eye**
aʊ	ab**ou**t, h**ow**
ɔɪ	v**oi**ce, b**oy**
ɪr	b**eer**
ɛr	b**are**
ɑr	b**ar**
ɔr	d**oor**
ʊr	t**our**

/t/ means that /t/ may be dropped.
/d/ means that /d/ may be dropped.
/ˈ/ shows main stress.
/ˌ/ shows secondary stress.
/◄/ shows stress shift.

Consonants

Symbol	Key Word
p	**p**ack, ha**pp**y
b	**b**ack, ru**bb**er
t	**t**ie
d	**d**ie
k	**c**ame, **k**ey, **qu**i**ck**
g	**g**ame, **g**uest
tʃ	**ch**ur**ch**, na**t**ure, wa**tch**
dʒ	**j**u**dg**e, **g**eneral, ma**j**or
f	**f**an, **ph**otogra**ph**
v	**v**an
θ	**th**ing, brea**th**
ð	**th**en, brea**the**
s	**s**ip, **c**ity, p**s**ychology
z	**z**ip, plea**s**e, goe**s**
ʃ	**sh**ip, ma**ch**ine, sta**ti**on, spe**ci**al, discu**ss**ion
ʒ	mea**s**ure, vi**s**ion
h	**h**ot, **wh**o
m	**m**en, so**m**e
n	su**n**, **kn**ow, **pn**eumonia
ŋ	su**ng**, ri**ng**ing
w	**w**et, **wh**ite
l	**l**ight, **l**ong
r	**r**ight, **wr**ong
y	**y**es, **u**se, m**u**sic
t̬	bu**tt**er, bo**tt**le
tˤ	bu**tt**on

Vocabulary Index

The numbers following each entry are the pages where the word appears. All words followed by asterisks* are on the Academic Word List.

flat /flæt/ 8, 9
follow /'falou/ 21, 22, 83, 90, 126, 139
fool /ful/ 125, 126, 127, 131, 166
form /fɔrm/ 101, 103, 139
forward /'fɔrwɚd/ 8, 9
frightened /'fraɪt̮nd/ 178, 179, 189
full /fʊl/ 34, 35, 42, 44, 146, 186
fun /fʌn/ 47, 48, 179

G

gardener /'gɑrdnɚ/ 173, 175
go free /gou 'fri/ 158, 160
grass /græs/ 15, 17, 22, 92, 93
ground /graʊnd/ 34, 35, 77, 93
guess /gɛs/ 96, 97
guilty /'gɪlti/ 158, 160, 189

H

hear about /'hɪʳr ə'baʊt/ 66, 67, 139, 175, 186
heat /hit/ 75, 77
hide /haɪd/ 164, 166, 189
historian /hɪ'stɔriən/ 178, 179
hit /hɪt/ 96, 97, 103, 160
hold on /hould 'ɔn/ 110, 112, 118, 151
hug /hʌg/ 66, 67, 93, 158, 160
humorous /'hyumərəs/ 53, 55
hunt /hʌnt/ 101, 103

I

identical* /aɪ'dɛn̮ɪkəl, ɪ-/ 145, 146, 150, 151, 186, 189
identify* /aɪ'dɛn̮ ə,faɪ, ɪ-/ 60, 62, 90, 189
identity* /aɪ'dɛn̮ ət̮i, ɪ-/ 130, 131, 146, 151, 189
illness /'ɪlnɪs/ 81, 83, 179
illusion /ɪ'luʒən/ 164, 166
image* /'ɪmɪdʒ/ 164, 166
imagine /ɪ'mædʒn/ 34, 35, 44, 48, 54, 55, 92, 103, 160, 166, 188
in advance /ɪn əd'væns/ 96, 97, 139
in case /ɪŋ 'kəɪs/ 150, 151
in fact /ɪn 'fækt/ 34, 35, 49, 54, 62, 97, 112, 131, 146, 151, 160, 179, 188, 189
independent /,ɪndɪ'pɛndənt◀/ 116, 118
inspect* /ɪn'spɛkt/ 150, 151
instead /ɪn'stɛd/ 116, 118, 126, 142, 160, 166
intelligence* /ɪn'tɛlədʒəns/ 81, 83
interpreter /ɪn'tɚprət̮ɚ/ 53, 54, 55
introduction /,ɪntrə'dʌkʃən/ 53, 54

J

joke /dʒouk/ 34, 35, 42

K

kick /kɪk/ 8, 9
knee /ni/ 150, 151

L

land /lænd/ 2, 3, 175
lawyer /'lɔyɚ/ 130, 131, 189
leader /'lidɚ/ 60, 62, 83
legal* /'ligəl/ 150, 151
license* /'laɪsəns/ 29, 31, 131
lie /laɪ/ 15, 17, 35, 125, 126, 160, 189
lie down /laɪ 'daʊn/ 145, 147
limit /'lɪmɪt/ 116, 118, 175
luck /lʌk/ 34, 35, 42, 62, 103, 112, 142

M

magician /mə'dʒɪʃən/ 164, 166
make fun of /meɪk 'fʌn əv/ 53, 55
market /'mɑrkɪt/ 173, 175
matching /'mætʃɪŋ/ 145, 146
meal /mil/ 15, 16, 22, 31, 44, 83
memory /'mɛmri, -məri/ 158, 160
mind /maɪnd/ 101, 103, 160, 179
mirror /'mɪrɚ/ 101, 103, 142
mistake /mɪ'steɪk/ 53, 55

N

natural /'nætʃərəl/ 8, 9, 16, 17, 75, 76, 90, 103, 127
nervous /'nɚvəs/ 101, 103
nest /nɛst/ 125, 126
nonsense /'nɑnsɛns, -səns/ 101, 103, 139

O

offensive /ə'fɛnsɪv/ 53, 54
opposite /'ɑpəzɪt, -sɪt/ 96, 97, 142
ordinary /'ɔrdn,ɛri/ 173, 175, 179, 188
organized /'ɔrgə,naɪzd/ 81, 83
owner /'ounɚ/ 66, 67

P

pass /pæs/ 29, 31, 97, 103, 131, 146
path /pæθ/ 81, 83
physical* /'fɪzɪkəl/ 53, 55, 179
pocket /'pɑkɪt/ 21, 23, 35, 42, 44, 131
poisonous /'pɔɪzənəs/ 29, 31
popular /'pɑpyəlɚ/ 47, 49, 55, 175, 186
power /'paʊɚ/ 8, 9, 17, 76, 166, 175, 179
practical /'præktɪkəl/ 29, 31, 62
predict* /prɪ'dɪkt/ 96, 97, 103
prepare /prɪ'pɛr/ 29, 31, 35, 44

MP3 Audio Tracking Guide